Cambridge Elements

Elements in Digital Literary Studies
edited by
Katherine Bode
Australian National University
Adam Hammond
University of Toronto
Gabriel Hankins
Clemson University

GENDER AND LITERARY GEOGRAPHY

Elizabeth F. Evans
Wayne State University

Matthew Wilkens
Cornell University

Shaftesbury Road, Cambridge CB2 8EA, United Kingdom

One Liberty Plaza, 20th Floor, New York, NY 10006, USA

477 Williamstown Road, Port Melbourne, VIC 3207, Australia

314–321, 3rd Floor, Plot 3, Splendor Forum, Jasola District Centre, New Delhi – 110025, India

103 Penang Road, #05-06/07, Visioncrest Commercial, Singapore 238467

Cambridge University Press is part of Cambridge University Press & Assessment, a department of the University of Cambridge.

We share the University's mission to contribute to society through the pursuit of education, learning and research at the highest international levels of excellence.

www.cambridge.org
Information on this title: www.cambridge.org/9781009571661

DOI: 10.1017/9781009029001

© Elizabeth F. Evans and Matthew Wilkens 2025

This publication is in copyright. Subject to statutory exception and to the provisions of relevant collective licensing agreements, no reproduction of any part may take place without the written permission of Cambridge University Press & Assessment.

When citing this work, please include a reference to the DOI 10.1017/9781009029001

First published 2025

A catalogue record for this publication is available from the British Library

ISBN 978-1-009-57166-1 Hardback
ISBN 978-1-009-01415-1 Paperback
ISSN 2633-4399 (online)
ISSN 2633-4380 (print)

Additional resources for this publication at www.cambridge.org/EvansWilkens

Cambridge University Press & Assessment has no responsibility for the persistence or accuracy of URLs for external or third-party internet websites referred to in this publication and does not guarantee that any content on such websites is, or will remain, accurate or appropriate.

For EU product safety concerns, contact us at Calle de José Abascal, 56, 1°, 28003 Madrid, Spain, or email eugpsr@cambridge.org

Gender and Literary Geography

Elements in Digital Literary Studies

DOI: 10.1017/9781009029001
First published online: April 2025

Elizabeth F. Evans
Wayne State University

Matthew Wilkens
Cornell University

Author for correspondence: Elizabeth Evans, e.f.evans@wayne.edu or Matthew Wilkens, wilkens@cornell.edu

Abstract: Our analysis of over 20,000 books published in Britain between 1800 and 2009 compares the geographic attention of fiction authored by women and by men; of books that focus on women and men as characters; and of works published in different eras. We find that, while there were only modest differences in geographic attention in books by men and women authors, there were dramatic geographic differences in books with highly gendered character space. Counter to expectation, the geographic differences between differently gendered characters were remarkably stable across these centuries. We also examine and complicate the power attributed to separate-sphere ideology. And we demonstrate a surprising reversal of critical expectation: in fiction, broadly natural spaces were more strongly associated with men, while urban spaces were more aligned with women. As it uncovers spatial patterns in literary history, this study casts new light on well-known texts and reimagines literature's broader engagement with gender and geography.

Keywords: literature, geography, gender, digital humanities, cultural analytics

© Elizabeth F. Evans and Matthew Wilkens 2025

ISBNs: 9781009571661 (HB), 9781009014151 (PB), 9781009029001 (OC)
ISSNs: 2633-4399 (online), 2633-4380 (print)

Contents

1 Introduction: Gender and Literary Geography 1

2 Gender and Language through Computation 9

3 Measuring Literary Space 17

4 Measuring Spatial Mobility 24

5 Geographic Intensity and Specificity 36

6 The Gendering of Public and Private Spaces 51

7 Gender and the City 68

8 Conclusions 80

Bibliography 84

1 Introduction: Gender and Literary Geography

The difference between men's and women's relationships with public space has long shaped literature, scholarship, and social life. It has structured narrative plots and character development and has been integral in the development of feminist theory, gender studies, and critical race theory. Contemporary social movements – from #MeToo to Black Lives Matter to Occupy – attest to the continuing, urgent relevance of physical space to cultural identities. Literary and cultural critics have sought to understand how social rules that structure the gendered occupation of space and the ability to travel, whether around the world or through a neighborhood, impact life and its representation. Yet little is known about how gender and representations of space interact at broad scale, across centuries and in many thousands of books.

Previous studies of gender and literary geography were restricted, by necessity, to individual books or small groups of texts.[1] That work has enriched immeasurably our understanding of the relationship between gender, space, and narrative (usually within a single literary era). But it lacks the scope to identify persistent patterns or to investigate the veracity of "common knowledge" narratives about literary geography that are widely shared, if often unstated.

The predominant but under-supported critical story is as follows: *in literature as in life, nineteenth- and early twentieth-century men had greater freedom of movement than did women. Men enjoyed greater access to urban environments, foreign locales, and public spaces, while women were more often confined to the home. Some gains in women's mobility were made in the early years of the twentieth century, but significant change did not come about until World War II, when women took up jobs left vacant by enlisted men. Aside from a conservative reaction in the 1950s, women's mobility thereafter increased until, in the late twentieth century, it approached that of men.*

The details of this sketch are debated, but, despite a paucity of evidence, its broad outlines remain unchallenged, even unquestioned. This story has had important effects, not only on the history of gender, but on such core concepts as "the city" and "nature." From its early days, metropolitan space, with its connotations of modernity, has been regarded as masculine, leading some to conclude that "The literature of modernity describes the experience of men. It is essentially a literature about transformations in the public world ... of work, politics and city life" from which women were excluded or "practically invisible."[2] Nature, on the other hand,

---

[1] The list of historians, geographers, and literary critics who have explored the intersection of gender and geography is long. Seminal work includes Nead, *Victorian Babylon*; Massey, *Space, Place, and Gender*; and Friedman, *Mappings*.
[2] Wolff, "Invisible Flâneuse," 37. For further discussion about Wolff's claim and its context, see Section 6.

bolstered by ancient conceptions of motherhood and fertility, has more often been represented as the preserve of the feminine.[3]

By examining the relationship between gender and geography in over 20,000 volumes of fiction published in Britain between 1800 and 2009, including special focus on the long modernist era near the middle of that period, we offer corrections to widespread assumptions about the role of gender in the geographic imagination. We identify how literary geography has changed – and remained consistent – over time and provide vital contexts for enriching our understanding of individual works of fiction. We also strive to detail how choices we made in the course of our research helped to shape our findings. As our discussion will emphasize, data collection and analysis are inevitably intertwined with human decision-making.

The remainder of this section surveys gender and literary geography in traditional literary studies, identifies the strengths and limits of quantitative methods in the field, and introduces the parameters of our investigation, including how our choices at the outset have shaped our research results.

1.1 Gender and Geography in Literary Studies: An Overview

Feminist literary criticism has always been alert to the significance of space in the construction of gender roles. As Virginia Woolf's *A Room of One's Own* (1929) famously argued, the spatial expression of gender roles has many implications for what and how literature was produced. Women's opportunities to become writers were – and perhaps still are – limited in two spatially constructed ways: women rarely enjoyed private space (the "room of one's own" necessary for sustained creative work), and they were denied access to particular places, from universities to certain parts of the city to foreign locations, that were foundational to male writers' development. While Woolf and her likeminded contemporaries saw unequal opportunities for men and women stretching back across centuries, it was to the Victorian era that they turned to explain the entrenchment of gender roles around spatial divisions. The ideology of separate spheres meant that men were duty-bound to brave the rough world of the public sphere, while women were obliged to create a sanctuary in the private home. As "the Angel in the House," to use the title of Coventry Patmore's hugely popular poem (first published in 1854), a proper (middle-class) woman would inhabit and produce domestic space, venturing alone into public spaces only to shop for her family or to conduct charitable visits to the homes of the poor.

---

[3] See Ortner, "Female to Male" for a succinct account of the long history of women's association with nature and men's association with culture.

However unevenly available and enforced separate sphere ideology was in practice, even after the end of Victoria's reign, it continued to delimit women's lives, as Woolf and others argued. Decades later, best-selling works of second-wave feminism such as Betty Friedan's *The Feminine Mystique* (1963) testified to its persistence. Literary scholars, from the 1970s onward, have explored how literature inculcated and policed gendered spatial divisions and how, alternatively, literature could help readers to imagine subverting those divisions.[4] The past generation of feminist literary scholarship has deepened its engagement with the spatial aspects of gender, examining not only how gender roles have been expressed, policed, and resisted spatially but also how the crucial roles of race, class, nationality, sexuality, age, ability, and other categories of identity intersect with gender in spatial organization.[5]

A key marker of social position is the availability and circumstances of travel. While people have always left (or been forced from) their homes to find new ones elsewhere – for work, for food, for a better life – the voluntary, temporary leaving of one's home is relatively new in human history and, until quite recently, one had to be very rich to afford it. It also helped if one were a man. The tradition of the Grand Tour arose in the seventeenth century as a necessary part of a wealthy young man's education, preparing him for his station as a political and social leader. Sending women abroad was generally regarded as a waste of money until the late nineteenth century, when finishing schools sprang up on the Continent to teach the daughters of elite families the skills that would help them secure a suitable husband. The nineteenth century in fact saw increasing numbers of women traveling abroad – for religious purposes, as the wives of colonial civil servants, and for education and pleasure – but they remained in the minority among travelers.[6] No wonder, then, that when women voyaged to more exotic lands, or traveled without chaperonage, they often seized the public's imagination. Florence Nightingale, Mary Kingsley, Gertrude Bell, the anthropologist Margaret Mead, and, earlier, Lady Mary Wortley Montagu were remarkable women travelers whose glamor derived in no small part from how very unusual they were. In the postwar era, the iconic woman traveler was a stewardess, whose mobility was largely confined to the airplane and its supporting spaces, the airport and the hotel. Even now, when international travel for wealthy Western women is a sign of their success,

---

[4] Foundational work includes Gilbert and Gubar, *Madwoman in the Attic*; Duplessis, *Writing beyond the Ending*; and Armstrong, *Desire and Domestic Fiction*.
[5] Patricia Hill Collins, Doreen Massey, and Katherine McKittrick are a few of the most influential feminist scholars to have pursued an intersectional analysis of gender and space.
[6] Studies of women and travel in the nineteenth and early twentieth centuries include Lawrence, *Penelope Voyages* and Kelley, *Excursions into Modernism*.

independent travel by women remains often a subject of special concern, as evinced by the near-obligatory "for the solo woman traveler" section in guidebooks and travel sites.

An area of intense scholarly interest has been the role of gender in two phenomena that are often conflated: the urban environment and modernity. In Britain, Europe, and North America, the great migration to cities initiated by the Industrial Revolution created a new way of life. In place of lives spent surrounded by familiar people, in landscapes known by their forbearers, large numbers of people experienced the shock of urban estrangement. The relative anonymity of the city and the dominance of industrial capitalism, with its timetables and quotas, made "modern life" distinct. Technological and cultural innovations from the telephone to the department store – and the changes in social relations they helped to bring about – generally reached cities first and in greater numbers. Travelers from foreign lands came first to cities, too, reinforcing the association of metropolitan life with global currents of trade, politics, and culture.[7]

Early scholarship on modernity and modernism largely neglected women's participation in the modern city.[8] Its literature, as it was constructed by literary critics of the 1960s, 1970s, and 1980s, largely celebrated the experience of the flâneur, the privileged man who walked the streets, observing closely under cover of his urban anonymity, and whose observation was rewarded with artistic inspiration. As an artist figure, the flâneur was linked both to modernity and to its representation. What, then, of the woman writer? Were flânerie and its artistic rewards available to her as well? Janet Wolff's argument that they were not provoked a flood of scholarship investigating the historical possibilities for women on urban streets and in other public places, along with a new interest in literature representing women's metropolitan experiences.[9] While the scholarly debate about the possibility of a flâneuse has subsided, there remains much interest among historians, literary scholars, and cultural critics in women's

---

[7] This summary of the widespread association of the urban environment with "modern life" is descriptive rather than prescriptive. The modern subject's sense of displacement and alienation, influentially theorized as a product of metropolitan life by Georg Simmel in 1903, was experienced earlier and more profoundly in non-urban locations by people taken from Africa as slaves, as Paul Gilroy argues in *The Black Atlantic*. Nor was provincial English life immune from modernity, as demonstrated in Bluemel and McCluskey, *Rural Modernity in Britain*.

[8] See Felski, *Gender of Modernity* for a critique of masculine-centered theories of modernity, particularly such influential work as Adorno and Horkheimer, *Dialectic of Enlightenment* and Berman, *All That Is Solid Melts into Air*.

[9] According to Wolff, women's estrangement from "the public world of work, politics and city life" (37) and their inability to share the "possibility and the prospect of lone travel, of voluntary uprooting, of anonymous arrival at a new place" (40) made flânerie unavailable to them. For subsequent scholarship, see especially Wilson, "Invisible Flâneur"; Nord, *Walking the Victorian Streets*; Walkowitz, *City of Dreadful Delight*; and Parsons, *Street Walking*.

Gender and Literary Geography 5

negotiation of urban space dominated by men in the nineteenth and twentieth centuries. Scholarship on the late twentieth- and twenty-first-century city has turned increasingly to gender's intersections with class, race, and global modernity, reflecting both an increasingly heterogeneous population and literary writers' engagement with that diversity.[10] Sexual harassment and the danger of sexual violence have continued to be horrifyingly relevant to representations of women's relationship with urban space.

Scholars have employed nuanced readings of individual literary texts to examine how gender informs the experience and representation of the urban environment and of space more broadly. These readings have paid substantial dividends for our understanding of certain texts. They are also the basis on which scholars have formed theories about larger patterns in literary history. If we want to understand the wider cultural terrain, however, we need to look beyond the relatively small number of texts that we read, write about, and teach. We need to examine the vast majority of books that are, to a greater or lesser degree, obscure to critical practice. Of course, we cannot read thousands of books as we would one or a dozen. But computational methods give us new evidentiary inroads to a series of questions that traditional forms of analysis cannot address in full – questions like: What difference does the gender of fictional characters make to their geographic mobility? How does an author's gender influence where a novel's characters travel? Are there differences in the kinds of places men and women authors represent in their fiction, and do those differences vary by the gender of their characters? How have the answers to all of these questions changed over time, from the early nineteenth century to the early twenty-first? This study uses the new affordances of computational methods, combined with more traditional modes of humanistic inquiry, to answer these and other questions of longstanding interest in literary and cultural studies.

1.2 The Texts in This Study

As with any literary study, it's important to understand the texts under analysis. We work with 21,347 books held by the HathiTrust digital library, the largest repository of digitized texts available for scholarly use. Our texts are the near entirety of the HathiTrust's holdings that we determined, through library metadata and other tools discussed at the end of this section, to be English-language fiction published in Britain between 1800 and 2009. They are the *near* entirety

---

[10] On nineteenth- and twentieth-century issues, see Sanders, *Consuming Fantasies*; Snaith, *Modernist Voyages*; Evans, *Threshold Modernism*; and Elkin, *Flâneuse*. For contemporary contexts, Dawson, *Mongrel Nation*; Ranasinha, *Contemporary Diasporic*; and essays in Hubble and Tew, *London in Contemporary British Fiction*.

in that we removed duplicate texts and any subsequent editions of popular works.

It's important to note the consequences of our choice not to include, so far as possible, multiple editions of a given work. Our goal was to allow each book equal weight in our analysis, so that volumes by minor and forgotten writers would "count" as much as those by canonical figures in English letters. We chose, in other words, to focus on the production and marketing of literature more than the consumption of literature. A different study would have resulted from a corpus that included multiple editions of single works, one that would more closely track the consumption of literature, but at the cost of decreasing the representation of minor voices. Despite our choice, canonical and widely popular texts do have slightly greater weight in our corpus than do other texts, for two reasons. First, they are more likely to have been reprinted in forms that our algorithm didn't detect: a novel might have been published under significantly different titles or with different author names over multiple centuries, or a popular author's books may have reappeared in collected forms that do not signal their specific content. Still, it's rare for a book to go even to a second edition, so the over-representation of canonical texts in this regard is fairly small (we estimate that between 0.9% and 2.8% of our titles are undetected reprints).

The second reason that canonical and pseudo-canonical texts are overrepresented in our corpus, despite our commitment to weighing equally all texts published in Britain, is that the academic libraries from which we source our texts are not equally likely to have collected every book. We chose to use HathiTrust's holdings to assemble our corpus because it offered the largest number of fictional volumes available for computational processing, providing an unprecedented collection of popular, largely forgotten novels, as well as most of the usual subjects of critical attention. It does not, however, include everything published in Britain, in part because the collection comes mostly from academic libraries in the United States.[11] The British Library probably comes closer to a comprehensive collection of the British publishing industry, including many texts that were never acquired by American educational institutions. Books published in Britain that never made it to American universities were likely disproportionately "popular" rather than literary, including childrens' books and pulp books, such as railway books, meant to be purchased, read

---

[11] The HathiTrust community comprises almost 250 libraries and academic consortia (such as the University of California and the Big Ten Academic Alliance). Of these, sixty-three have contributed to HathiTrust's digitized holdings. Our data set includes volumes sourced from twenty-three different libraries. For a list of Hathi contributors, see the HathiTrust summary of volumes contributed. For a list of volumes and sources in our data set, see the online supplementary materials to this Element (https://github.com/wilkens/gender-and-literary-geography).

once, and discarded. The British Library, however, despite a large-scale digitization program, has not made its texts publicly available for computational research. It is also the case that not all authors enjoyed equal access to formal publication. Even if our corpus did include every published book, there would exist a significant body of narrative fiction excluded due to the biases and priorities of the historical publishing industries.[12] We must, as Doris Lessing cautioned, "remember that for all the books we have in print, [there] are as many that have never reached print, have never been written down" (*Golden Notebook*, xxiv).

There is some evidence that the particular qualities of a sample of historical literary texts may make less difference than is often imagined. Research by Ted Underwood, Patrick Kimutis, and Jessica Witte comparing differently constructed subsets of fiction volumes drawn from the HathiTrust library shows that, for a wide range of problems, "trends of interest to researchers follow many of the same diachronic arcs," suggesting that at least some patterns are "too durable to be purely an artifact of library collection practices."[13] Further, comparisons of HathiTrust's collection with corpora assembled from other sources – *Publishers Weekly*, for example, or a manually assembled corpus of novels available from diverse sources – showed similar trends in author and character gender composition over time (Underwood, Bamman, and Lee, "Transformations of Gender," 3–7).

Further choices deserve comment. This study uses only works published in English, including translations of foreign-language books (we estimate between 9% and 10% of included volumes are translations, mostly from Western European languages). One could eliminate some of the translations via bibliographic metadata, but we have not attempted to do so, because we seek to survey as much of the British fiction market as possible. We want, in other words, to assess the books that were available to Anglophone British readers, regardless of their provenance. A different choice might have produced different results, though we have no evidence to suggest that translated books are necessarily different from nontranslated books in the dimensions of interest to us. Works published in Britain are of course not the same as works written by British authors, but there is a high degree of overlap (about 80% in our corpus,

---

[12] For discussion of the partiality of the archive, see Engel and Ruth, "Women and Archives" and Brown and Mandell, "The Identity Issue."
[13] Underwood, Kimutis, and Witte, "NovelTM Datasets for English-Language Fiction, 1700–2009," 5. For additional considerations of the relationships between archival sources, see Ryan and Ahnert, "The Measure of the Archive" and Algee-Hewitt, Allison, Gemma, et al., "Canon/Archive."

according to our estimates, though the fraction varies over time; see also Wilkens, "Too Isolated").

It's important to acknowledge that fiction is surprisingly difficult to detect. Libraries did not begin classifying genre until the late twentieth century. Even now, library metadata is inconsistent in labeling early books as "fiction" or "nonfiction." According to Underwood, Kimutis, and Witte, a sample of pre-1900 fiction that relied purely on metadata "would leave out more than half of the fiction, and it might be biased specifically against obscure writers" (3; see also Underwood, "Understanding Genre"). Our identification of "fiction" is drawn from Underwood et al.'s algorithmic predictions over the whole of the HathiTrust library, setting our selection cutoff at volumes predicted to be no less than 80% likely to contain at least 80% fiction content. This probabilistic method means that our corpus erroneously excludes some fiction volumes and includes others that skilled human readers would not classify as fiction, though these are often marginal cases such as memoir, biography, travelogue, and narrative history. We begin our study in 1800 because HathiTrust's coverage is sparse and uneven before that. We end our study in 2009, the most recent year available. Underwood, Kimutis, and Witte, in "NovelTM Datasets for English-Language Fiction, 1700–2009," provide a rich discussion of the makeup of the HathiTrust collection.

1.3 Overview of Research Results

At the beginning of this section, we summarized the popular, if undersupported, critical consensus about the intersection of gender and literary geography over the past two centuries. This set of expectations imagines literature reflecting Western women's increasing mobility over time as they moved out of the home and traveled more extensively beyond it. In opposition to this critical consensus, we demonstrate that books by men and women *authors* over the past two centuries of British literature showed relatively little difference in their characters' overall mobility. The mobility of men and women *characters*, however, diverged much more sharply and the gap between them remained surprisingly consistent over time. We theorize that literary geography functioned less as a reflection of gender-determined differences in authors' personal experience than as an index of other cultural forces that shaped conventionally masculine and feminine roles, such as the availability of formal education and opportunities for economic independence. In other words, authors expressed a multitude of constraints for women *through* geographic limitations for their characters. While opportunities for travel opened up to women over time, the ongoing constraint of women characters at the turn of the twenty-first century suggests that the physical world is not yet seen as fully available for women's exploration. Furthermore, while we do find evidence of the doctrine of separate spheres – women authors and characters were more aligned with the home and male authors and characters were more aligned with streets and other public byways – we discover a surprising reversal of expectations in urban and natural spaces. In the British fiction we examine, cities were associated most frequently with women, while rural and natural spaces were most affiliated with men. This finding provides an opportunity not only to reevaluate the critical conflations of urban modernity with masculinity and of nature with women but to trace their roots in the history of textual acquisition and canon formation.

We will have much more to say about all of these findings in the sections ahead. But first, we must make a short detour through the mechanics of our work and the intellectual considerations they raise.

2 Gender and Language through Computation

As we noted in Section 1, this study involves 21,347 volumes of fiction published in Britain between 1800 and 2009 and digitized by the HathiTrust library consortium. Our work relies on two different types of information extracted from these books. The first concerns their use of spatial and geographic references. We'll have more to say about that data in Section 3. The second concerns the gender performances of the books' authors and characters. Here, we describe the process by which gender information was collected and the range of limitations attached to it.

There are two important points to make before we dig into the details of our gender data. First, we note that, like much research in digital humanities, our work is the product of many hands. The data we use concerning the gender identities of authors and characters in our corpus was produced by Ted Underwood, David Bamman, and Sabrina Lee and was originally used in their article "The Transformation of Gender in English-Language Fiction." We cannot recommend that article highly enough to anyone who cares about the history of gender and literature.[14] Of course, responsibility for the accuracy of the data we use and for the suitability of the methods by which it was produced lie with us, even in cases where we weren't the ones who wrote or ran the original code that produced it. We have made some small changes around the margins of the Underwood et al. dataset, and some much larger

---

[14] For additional results and reflection on the application of quantitative methods to questions of literary gender, see Brown and Mandell, as well as Jockers and Kiriloff, "Understanding Gender." For productive attempts to introduce multidimensional models of performed identity in narrative text, see Bamman, Underwood, and Smith, "A Bayesian Mixed Effects Model of Literary Character" and Piper, *Enumerations*, ch. 5.

ones involving corpus selection, but when we describe the methods in this section, we want to be careful not to claim credit for the labor of others.

We believe that there are substantial benefits to working with existing data where possible. Beyond the practical advantages of efficiency and accessibility, using standard datasets helps to build a library of results that draw on shared resources. These results, in turn, help other researchers better understand the data and its limits, and they lend credibility to a baseline against which new work and new datasets can be evaluated. As quantitative methods spread more widely in the humanities, the value of widely used, well understood, and carefully vetted datasets, especially those linked to the HathiTrust library, seems certain to grow. That said, no dataset, no matter how well established, stands on its own. As we discuss in the next subsections, the data we use – whether produced directly by us or borrowed from others – is the product of human decisions, cultural processes, and technical constraints that stretch backward from our own desks through academic laboratories, cultural institutions, commercial concerns, and social formations over decades and centuries.

The second high-level point is that the model of gender we use for both authors and characters is partially binary, though our data allow us to treat a given book as occupying a position along a continuum between feminine and masculine. Each author and each fictional character in our corpus is labeled man, woman, or unknown. We make no algorithmic attempt to further divide or refine individual gender identities in our data. We do so because we believe that there are substantial benefits to working with these high-level, historically salient categories. Large-scale analysis of binary gender construction's textual effects helps to reveal historical inequities and areas of gender convergence that may not match our critical expectations. It can also illuminate new aspects of the historical construction of gender and new aspects of literature's role in gender performance. This is to say that binary approaches to classification, in combination with nonbinary aggregation of gendered characteristics, can do more to produce nuance than to undermine it. When we look at the "masculine-coded" and "feminine-coded" allocations of textual space, we discover that practically no book is all one or the other.

It should be obvious that we are not concerned on any occasion with biological sex. In the social realm of gender, our focus is on the aggregate interaction of individual performances with historically evolving positions. To minimize confusion on this point, and in keeping with current practice in gender studies, we generally avoid the adjectives *female* and *male*, preferring *women* and *men* or, rarely, *feminine* and *masculine*.

2.1 Methods: Author Gender

We examine the genders of both authors and fictional characters in our corpus. Each book that we study thus has at least two gender attributes: the (binary) gender of its author and the (nonbinary) fraction of narrative space devoted to men and women characters. Both of these attributes are derived directly from the data released by Underwood, Bamman, and Lee.

To assess authorial gender, Underwood et al. used US census records to match authors' first names with prevailing use at the time of publication.[15] While British census records would have been preferable for our purposes, we find no evidence of large, systematic differences in the gender associations of first names between the United States and Britain over the last two centuries. Well-known cases of women authors who used male pseudonyms (i.e., George Eliot, George Sand) were hand-corrected, but there are surely other, less familiar cases that slipped through. There is an argument to be made that authors who chose to publish under a name with marked gender associations shouldn't be "corrected" at all, since an author's chosen name is a significant part of the gender performance of the text. But in the handful of prominent cases where we have overridden the gender implied by a pseudonym (as with Mary Ann Evans/ George Eliot and Charlotte Brontë/Currer Bell), the author's gender was widely known soon after the publication of their first novels. Names missing from the census records, including those identified only with initials, were assigned "unknown" gender. These books (3,358 in total, 15.7% of the corpus) were excluded from some of our analyses, but remain in the corpus and are included in cases where we do not focus on authorial gender. The composition of the full corpus by author gender is 30% women, 54% men, and (as noted) roughly 16% authors of unknown gender, though these percentages vary over time.

Census records are an imperfect proxy for author gender, of course. They are, moreover, inconsistently imperfect. Names missing from the census records, and therefore excluded, are more likely to be of non-Anglo origin. We therefore can expect that the corpus of books with an identified authorial gender may skew somewhat more Anglo-American in authorship than our original HathiTrust fiction corpus as a whole. This has the effect of making our "British" books – by which we mean books published in Britain – more likely to be "British" in the sense of being written by an author identified as British.

Straightforward errors – where an author's name signals a gender that is inconsistent with the known historical record and where we might have wished to rectify the discrepancy – are possible but infrequent. In a few

---

[15] Specifically, Underwood et al. used Bridget Baird and Cameron Blevins' "Gender ID by Time" package, with limited hand corrections of prominent authors.

cases, a name once associated with men became ambiguous or given primarily to women, as has been the case with Alexis, Ashley, and Kim, but these are mostly handled by the historical nature of the name-lookup data. Errors are slightly more likely to occur when we've mistaken the date of first publication – when, for example, a reprint is misidentified as the original publication, sending the algorithm to search the census in the wrong period. But there are relatively few reprints in our corpus and even fewer gender-evolving names. Names that might refer to either a man or woman holder in a single historical moment (e.g., Evelyn, Claire, Sidney) are labeled "unknown," the method requiring over 80% of a single gender to declare a result.

Overall, the accuracy of authorial gender prediction is better than we might have feared. Among authors, men are identified with precision of 0.99 and recall of 0.83, while women show better recall (0.90) but somewhat worse precision (0.91, still pretty good). *Precision* refers to the fraction of labeled instances that are correct; here, for example, among all the authors labeled women, 91% are indeed women, as determined by biographical research. *Recall* refers to the fraction of all instances in the data that are labeled correctly; in our case, for example, among all the authors in the corpus who should have been labeled women, we catch 90% of them. Authors labeled with unknown gender are, in a sample of cases where historical research is able to identify a gender, significantly more likely to be men than women (78.2% men, compared to 64.5% men among volumes with algorithmically labeled author gender). There is thus no evidence that women authors in our corpus were disproportionately likely to publish under gender-obscuring pseudonyms or initialisms.

2.2 Methods: Character Gender

The perceived gender of its author is one facet of a book's gender performance. Another concerns the fictional characters within the book. To assess the latter, we used a modified version of Underwood et al.'s character gender data. Broadly speaking, this data was produced by identifying the characters present in a book, labeling all the words associated with each character, and inferring the gender of each character by reference to the gender-indicating words associated with it (pronouns and honorifics, for the most part). This data allows us to assign a gender "score" to each book, which measures the fraction of overall narrative attention devoted to women characters.

Character gender data was the product of a natural language processing pipeline called BookNLP, developed by David Bamman and built on standard natural language processing (NLP) tools used in computer science and

Gender and Literary Geography 13

computational linguistics.[16] To infer the probable binary gender of each character, BookNLP uses pronouns and gender-indicating honorifics, such as Mr., Mrs., Sir, and Lady. In effect, nearly all characters are gendered according to the pronouns and titles they use in a way that mirrors contemporary social practice. In cases where such direct evidence of gender performance is absent or ambiguous, the algorithm also considers low-noise historical name data. Because "I" does not unambiguously indicate gender, first-person narrators are not included, nor does the algorithm catch characters who aren't given proper names, such as "teacher" or "the shopgirl." But the process does produce good results. Underwood et al. report that women are identified with 94.7% precision/83.1% recall and men are identified with 91.3% precision/85.7% recall. While the algorithm fails to find 16.9% of women characters and 14.3% of men characters, when found, a character's gender attribution matches what human readers would assign in over 90% of cases. Even more importantly, both for the arguments Underwood et al. present and for the arguments this Element will make, accuracy is relatively stable over time (3).[17]

George Eliot's *Middlemarch* (1871–72) provides a typical example of the method's performance. Gender is correctly assigned to the major characters – Dorothea, Lydgate, Mr. Casaubon, and so forth – and we measure the fraction of narrative space (see later in this section) devoted to women at 0.371. This result may surprise readers who remember Dorothea as the novel's protagonist, but it captures the book's overall distribution of character space by (binary) gender.

There are obvious constraints imposed by this method, however. Chief among them is that we miss gender ambiguity. The pronoun "he" will trigger a male label no matter the character's personal sense of gender identity. If the text calls Roger a man, a man he will be. An example helps us consider the implications of this fact. Radclyffe Hall, author of the important early queer bildungsroman *Well of Loneliness*, wrote a short story, "Miss Ogilvy Finds Herself" (1926/34), in which the protagonist is described as deeply uncomfortable in a woman's body and conventional roles. Assigned female at birth, Ogilvy insisted as a child "that her real name was William and not Wilhelmina" (6). While, throughout her life, "Miss Ogilvy" struggles internally with the dissonance between her felt and attributed gender, the text continues to

---

[16] For a full description of BookNLP, see Bamman, Underwood, and Smith. As of 2023, there is a new version of BookNLP; we did not use this newer version, but it would be a starting point for future work along similar lines.

[17] Characters of unknown gender are generally excluded from our study. There are quite a few of these (28.5% of all identified characters), but they tend to be minor and account for only a small fraction (8.7%) of the average book's character space. This makes sense: minor characters are, by definition, the characters least likely to possess gender-indicating details such as titles and pronouns.

use feminine pronouns and the feminine title "Miss" to describe her, with one notable exception: pronouns shift to he/him in a sequence in which Ogilvy either dreams of or temporarily becomes (the text is ambiguous) the man she was in a previous life "thousands and thousands of years ago" (22). Because this prehistoric man is not named, he would not be identified in our study as a character, while Miss Ogilvy would simply be identified as a woman character. While our process flattens the much more complex and nuanced account of gender produced by the story, it does accurately capture the way in which she is labeled by the majority of the text and by the fictional world around her. Critics have followed the text in using she/her pronouns for Miss Ogilvy.

Gendered character-space is a measure of how much of a book concerns the lives of women and girls and of how much of it concerns the lives of men and boys. "Character-space" refers to those portions of a fictional book that are concerned with identified characters and words connected with those characters.[18] A character's "space" includes the words used to narrate the actions they perform, the actions of which they are the objects, the adjectives that modify them, the nouns they possess, and the words they speak. We weighed each of these five ways of occupying fictional space equally. Our character-based gender score is then simply the amount of weighted character space devoted to women and girls, divided by the total gender-assigned character space of the book. A book that devotes exactly the same amount of attention to men and women characters would have a gender score of 0.5, or 50% women. We termed this score the "absolute" gender score of the text. For reference, Virginia Woolf's novel *Mrs. Dalloway* (1925) measures close to even distribution of character space by gender (at 53% women).

As we noted earlier, an advantage of this book-level scoring method is that it allows us to treat a book as a mixture of masculine and feminine characterization, acknowledging and working with a continuum of literary gender performance even within a framework of binary character-level gender attribution. In some cases, we found it useful to compare books closer to the poles of gendered character space. But this left us with an interpretive dilemma. The books in our corpus contain, on average, significantly more character space devoted to men than to women (about twice as much, in fact). If we define the poles of character space in absolute terms (at 75% men or women, for instance), we will have many more books centered on men than on women (about 10 to 1 at that level), reflecting (accurately) the general hyperallocation of character space to men over the last 200 years.[19]

---

[18] We borrow the term from Underwood et al., who adapt it from Woloch, *The One Versus the Many*. An analogous term from media studies is "screentime."

[19] Underwood, Bamman, and Lee trace in detail the dynamics of character-space allocation and speculate on their underlying causes.

Gender and Literary Geography

The stark difference in degrees of attention given to men and women characters is important here because it means that if we want to compare predominantly feminine texts and predominantly masculine texts by gender score alone, we would necessarily work with wildly different subcorpus sizes. The number of books in our corpus that have a gender score of at least 75% (mostly women) is just 746 (out of 21,347 volumes), compared to 8,528 books that have a gender score lower than 25% (mostly men). The quantity of women-centered books is enough for analyses of the period as a whole (1800–2009), but is generally not enough to produce high levels of statistical confidence when we split those 746 books into subsets by narrower time periods.[20] Comparing the size of these highly gender-skewed groups is a useful exercise in itself to appreciate this aspect of the sexist history of the book trade (Figure 1). It provides a vivid indication of whose stories have been deemed worth writing, reading, publishing, acquiring (by academic libraries), and preserving. One hopes it also provides motivation to change those practices.

To address the problem of small samples and to implement an alternative critical model of what it means for a book to be oriented toward women characters, we took the top and bottom 20% of books ranked by character space. (We might have chosen a different cut point, of course.) Doing so gave us equal numbers of each (4,270 volumes in each class, to be exact), but set different limits of what it means for a book to be "mostly about men" (no more than 13% of character space devoted to women, in practice) or "mostly about women" (not less than 53% of character space devoted to women). To put this another way, texts that devote over 53% of their attention to women and girls are, by historical standards, highly women-centered, even when they devote nearly as much character space to men as to women. When, in subsequent sections, we analyze books that are "mostly about women" (or men) or that "skew toward women" (or men), these top and bottom 20% subsets are the groups to which we refer. On no occasion do we simply divide the corpus at the 50% level.

We selected the top and bottom 20% of books as measured across the entire corpus. This means that our two character-space subcorpora are of equal size and consistent meaning over the period, even as the historically contingent meaning of a women-centered work changed. (In some periods, the top 20% of books were less women-centered than at other periods.) This means that our two subcorpora do not represent all time periods equally. The women-centered books contain somewhat fewer books from the 1940–70 period, for example,

---

[20] Readers interested in exploring books with such extremes of gender representation may find several lists in the associated data repository.

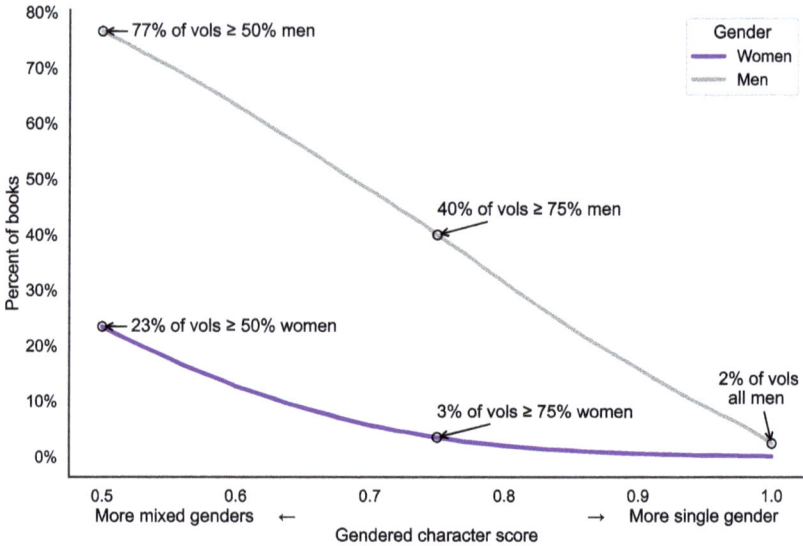

Figure 1 Varying the definition of "mostly women" and "mostly men." A plot of the percent of books in the corpus as a function of the computed character space score, grouped by predominant gender. Less than 25% of books are majority-women by this metric. Less than 5% are above three quarters women. Compare the male case: 75% of books devote the majority of their character space to men; 40% devote more than three quarters to men.

since books published in those decades devoted an even smaller fraction of their character space to women than was the norm across the nineteenth and twentieth centuries.

In short, there is no way to measure or subdivide our way out of the gender inequality of the last two hundred years of literary history. But we can choose different ways to assess that inequality, depending on which of its aspects we seek to understand. In the next section, we'll see a similar phenomenon concerning the distribution of spatial attention in the corpus. We'll also consider what's involved in extracting geographic references from billions of words of literary narrative, what we can learn from patterns of literary geography, and what challenges we face when we try to map colloquial, historical, and imaginary places to specific coordinates on a globe. Just as we have found in the case of literary gender, measuring textual geography is possible only at the confluence of intellectual and practical concerns. Quantitative work is very much like conventional criticism in this way: we make assumptions, we set bounds, and we read, always, under constraints that enable us to make specific, situated claims.

3 Measuring Literary Space

If you've seen one piece of scholarship in the digital humanities or one DH project, there's a good chance it involved a map. The maps and cartograms in Moretti's *Graphs, Maps, Trees* help to identify social relationships and modes of spatial narration in nineteenth-century literature. Stanford's *Mapping the Republic of Letters* produced what may be the most frequently seen DH visualization of the last two decades in their orange-on-black network map of eighteenth-century European correspondence (Edelstein et al.). Dozens of one-off projects include Google-based static and interactive maps of significant locations in specific novels or connected to the lives of individual authors.[21] Maps, it is safe to say, are a signature visual form of modern digital humanities.

Why is this? Why are maps so popular today when they were (and remain) rarely present in analog scholarship? The reasons are several. For one, paper maps are good to think with, but hard to publish. For all the Joyceans who have maps of Dublin on the walls of their offices, covered in color-coded pins that mark significant locations, how many have translated those scholarly devices into camera-ready, rights-cleared, publisher-approved illustrations? Who owns the rights to the base map? How much does that entity charge to republish it? How does one scale a full-color wall map of a square meter or more into a grayscale version legible at a quarter page? It has often thus proven (much) easier to describe in words a geospatial pattern identified on a map than it has been to display that pattern graphically.

Digital maps solve, or at least ameliorate, most of these practical problems, especially when the ultimate publication format is itself digital. Base maps from OpenStreetMap and (with some hand waving) from Google, Microsoft, Stamen, Mapbox, and others are freely available to academics. Web mapping interfaces handle scaling fairly well, support colors, are familiar from readers' daily use, are generally suitable for collaborative use, and can be embedded within most digital publishing platforms. With a little more experience (or help from a university's digital scholarship center), digital maps also work well with georectified archival basemaps, which can be important for historical work.

Maps are excellent exploratory tools, and digital maps solve a lot of the practical problems previously inherent in scholarly map use. Hence their ubiquity in digital scholarship. But maps' range of potential applicability is narrower than one might imagine, even for work that is explicitly concerned with

---

[21] For examples of such projects, see Cooper, Donaldson, and Murrieta-Flores eds., *Literary Mapping*.

literary geography. Maps are, for the most part, mesoscale devices, best deployed in service of a moderate amount of text. They work well at the scale of the book or the small collection (poets' travels in the English Lake District or Faulkner's Yoknapatawpha novels, for instance), where they can help to surface patterns of use that might otherwise escape readers' attention. But maps can lose value at larger scales, where they become both visually overloaded and, in many cases, recapitulate other aspects of human geography (population density, for example, or topography).

The affinity between mapping and mesoscale collections helps to explain the early rise and continued relevance of cartography as a DH technique. Digital maps are computationally tractable, manageable by individual researchers, and appropriate to the kinds of collections with which many literary scholars are comfortable (and on which those scholars can lay hands via general-purpose resources like Project Gutenberg or specialized collections like the Whitman Archive). But you won't find any maps in this Element, because the patterns we care about – the patterns of geographic usage that are relevant to the study of thousands of books published over more than two centuries – are not primarily visual in the sense encoded by maps. These patterns are instead temporal, demographic, political and, above all, statistical: how characters were distributed within and outside Britain over decades, or the differing associations between specific places and character genders in the work of men and women authors, or the shifting gender use of non-geographic spaces in urban and rural settings across historical events.

To identify and study these patterns requires bulk extraction of geospatial information from our corpus. This extraction is difficult and prone to certain errors, just as is the gender identification pipeline we described in Section 2. What we detail in Section 3.1 is how we carry it out, the underlying theory of the process, where some of the limits of the derived data lie, and how very recent developments in natural language processing methods do (and do not) offer the prospect of future improvements in the accuracy of the overall approach.

The remainder of this section will be most useful to those who want to follow the details of our method, whether to understand its affordances, to reproduce our results, or to carry out similar research on their own. Our aim has been to present technical material in accessible language. While some readers may prefer to skip directly to Section 4 – which they may do without overlooking substantive results – the information in the rest of this section will help to make clear the ways in which our investigation has been shaped by the tools at our disposal.

3.1 Spatial and Geolocation Extraction Methods

The first, and easiest, way to identify spatial and geographic references in unstructured text is to look for specific words that indicate places of interest.[22] We can find every instance of the generic terms like "street" or "bedroom," for example, or of specific place names like "London" and "France," provided we know in advance the words that are relevant to our problem. Indeed, we use this method for a subset of our results, especially in those cases where our interest is in space and spatial types (streets, domestic interiors) rather than in geography.

There are several important limitations to such dictionary-based methods. Most significantly, word counts do not cope well with polysemy. The noun "park" (a public green space) and the verb "park" (to stop and leave a vehicle) – to say nothing of a car park – are distinguished not by their orthography, but by their context. A version of the same problem holds for some geographic references, too. "Charlotte" might be a person or an American city. "Cambridge" is (almost) certainly a city, but is it British or American? We discuss these problems and our solutions to them in detail below.

Another limitation is practical. We source the digital texts in our corpus from the HathiTrust digital library. For volumes that are out of copyright, we can store and query the full text of each book locally, using whatever computational methods and resources are available to us. This makes it relatively quick and easy to perform iterative experiments (changing word lists, retaining or eliminating capitalization, identifying multi-word target terms ["car park," "New York City"], and so on) on these public-domain texts. But Hathi cannot, for legal reasons, release to researchers (or to the public) the full text of in-copyright volumes. Unfortunately, in-copyright volumes make up a large portion (about half) of the books in our corpus. Specifically, nearly all the books in our corpus that were originally published after the early 1920s remain in copyright.

To work with in-copyright volumes – and thus to extend our study through most of the twentieth and twenty-first centuries – we have three options, each of which is useful, but none of which is perfect. We use each of these options for parts of our study.

1. We can use the HathiTrust Research Center's (HTRC) extracted features dataset (Jett et al.). This dataset contains page-level bags of words (i.e., a list of the unique words that occur on a given page of a volume), each tagged

---

[22] When the target words are geographic, this approach is called gazetteering, from the term describing a geographic index or dictionary. Unstructured text is what readers encounter every day: ordinary natural language writing that has not been parsed or marked up for computational use.

with its computationally inferred part of speech (POS), along with the number of times the word-POS pair appeared on that page. The extracted features lose word order, which rules out many advanced analysis methods and simple counts of multi-word terms, but they have the merit of being freely available for local use and of covering the entirety of our corpus, including in-copyright volumes.

2. We can work with the HTRC's data capsule system. These are remote computers that allow offline access to the full text of all Hathi volumes. What this means is that researchers can write analysis code to be run against Hathi's full holdings on the HTRC's systems. The output of that code is then reviewed by HTRC staff to ensure that it does not leak copyright-protected content (by writing out the full text of in-copyright volumes, for example) and, once cleared, the results are supplied back to the researcher. This is a good system for small- to medium-scale projects, but it's hard to use for larger ones. It places significant strain on HTRC staff who review outputs. It is flatly unusable for outputs that are too large for realistic human review. It limits the computational power available to the equivalent of a single desktop, and it slows down iterative development by introducing time-consuming manual legal compliance review of every output. The data capsules are an excellent solution to a difficult legal problem for smaller projects, and we have used them in select cases, but they aren't intended to replace direct access for large-scale work.

3. Finally, for library-scale work that includes in-copyright volumes, we can collaborate with HTRC developers to run our code on the HTRC's full compute resources. This, too, involves human review of code and outputs, plus the significant overhead inherent in any research collaboration, but it allows us to run targeted, high-value (to us), computationally intensive workflows on a one-off basis, with outputs that we can then store locally for later analysis. This is the route we followed in devising and implementing the Textual Geographies project (txtgeo.net), which is the source of most of the geographic data we use in the present work.

We have used each of these access methods for parts of our study. We focus here on the third option, algorithmic extraction of named geographic locations from the full corpus, which we carried out in necessary collaboration with HTRC staff including Guangchen Ruan, Boris Capitanu, and Beth Plale. The second option is technically similar, though smaller in scale. We discuss the first option in more detail in Sections 6 and 7, in conjunction with those parts of our work that make extensive use of generic spatial terms rather than geographic data.

Gender and Literary Geography

As we noted early in this section, polysemy is a problem for many dictionary-based methods. To address the uncertainties of textual reference to geographic locations, we implemented a multistep pipeline that first identified words and sequences of words in books that were used, in context, as geographic references.[23] These might include, for example, real and well-known places like "Berlin" or "Los Angeles," but also obscure, fictional, or extraterrestrial locations ("Moon," "Heaven," "Yoknapatawpha County"). Our system relied on a conditional random field named entity recognition algorithm of the type introduced by Lafferty, McCallum, and Periera and implemented by Finkel et al. as part of the Stanford NLP toolset. Full details for the technically inclined are in the original papers, but the idea is that one can predict the role or meaning of a given word in context by examining the handful of words around it and comparing them to the words around other target terms of known type. Such an inference is a form of supervised learning; it depends on labeled training data to build the set of probabilities from which the algorithm makes its predictions. In more personifying terms, the algorithm learns not only that some words are used (almost) exclusively as place names, but also that phrases like "travel from ... " or "in the city of ... " are strong predictors that the next word (or words) will be a location (especially if capitalized). The algorithm thus also "knows" the difference between "a flight from Charlotte" and "my friend Charlotte" and can classify each "Charlotte" as a different type of named entity.

Naturally, predictive named entity recognition of this type is imperfect. Its accuracy depends on the regularities of the training data from which it extracts its contextual probabilities. If the training data is very different from the text on which the model is applied, that is, if the target text contains many terms or constructs that the model has never seen, the model's accuracy will suffer. Poetic, catachrestic, and anachronistic language use poses special challenges (as it does for human readers). Existing statistical models are generally trained on contemporary nonfiction, rather than on the historical literary sources that make up, to a greater or lesser degree, our corpus, so our case is an especially challenging one. In fact, we tested a new model trained on nineteenth-century literary texts in an attempt to improve performance on the texts in our corpus. But we found that the larger size of the pretrained models supplied by Finkel et al., combined with the perhaps underappreciated historical stability of relevant aspects of English usage, led to superior accuracy when employing the stock models alone.

---

[23] Our geographic dataset is available in the online repository for this Element. Additional data, covering more than 9 million volumes on all subjects, written in English, Spanish, German, and Chinese is available from the Textual Geographies project (txtgeo.net).

Readers familiar with recent developments in natural language processing may note that another approach to improving the performance of our system would involve using a large neural language model such as BERT or its many descendants to perform named entity recognition, perhaps fine-tuning on the literary training data that proved inadequate as the basis for a standalone model. Indeed, David Bamman and his group at Berkeley released such a system, an updated version of BookNLP, after our work was substantially complete.[24] These language models implement a form of transfer learning, in which model parameters learned from very large corpora provide a base representation that is then refined for a particular task and corpus. If we were beginning this research from scratch, there is no doubt that a large language model would be our point of departure. But the extra five or so percentage points of NER accuracy we would gain, while very welcome, are no panacea. We haven't yet discussed the geolocation and hand correction steps that lie downstream from entity recognition and that have a significant impact on the overall performance of the system. Large language models, especially of the scale necessary to achieve the most impressive performance, are also expensive to train and to use, requiring specialized compute hardware to complete their calculations in acceptable time.[25] And there is, as of this writing, no possibility of using such models with in-copyright Hathi texts. In short, while a move to large language models wasn't tenable for this project today, researchers in the field should be aware that such methods exist, and that they are the default starting point for most new work. Those researchers should also remain cognizant of the rapid pace of change in contemporary NLP, which is a source of both great excitement and of some disorientation.

Named entity recognition provides us with a list of the locations used in each volume. These locations range from the very specific (a building or business, a city square) to the very general (nations and continents), include both real and fictional places, and include a large number of variant names, spellings, and colloquial usages. To treat these locations as parts of a geographic system, we need to associate each of them with harmonized geographic and political data. We need to know, for instance, that Trafalgar Square is a public square located at 51.5080390° latitude, −0.1280690° longitude in the city of Westminster, which is part of the city (but not the City) of London, which is a locality in the district of Greater London, which is part of the top-level administrative area of England, which is part of the nation of the United Kingdom of Great Britain and Northern Ireland, which is, geographically at least, part of Europe. For most places, there is

---

[24] See Bamman, Popat, and Shen, "Annotated Dataset" and github.com/booknlp.

[25] A recent trial run of a BERT-based NER system on 100,000 Hathi texts required two weeks of distributed cloud compute runtime at a cost of more than $5,000. Costs are higher for more advanced models.

a simple, one-to-one or many-to-one mapping between a set of names by which a location may be referred and its canonical geopolitical data. We retrieve these mappings via Google's Places and Geocoding services. The Places API is the comparatively expensive one, which knows that "Constantinople" and "Istanbul" refer to a historically continuous city-level entity and that "Londan" is almost certainly a typo (or digitization error) for "London." From the Places API, we retrieve a set of probabilistically ranked unique identifiers for the geospatial entities to which a given string might refer. In most cases, we accept the most likely entity and use the Geocoding API to associate it with detailed geographic data. For relatively high-frequency places with significant ambiguity ("Cambridge" or "Richmond," for example, but not "Paris," because the instances in which a book uses "Paris" to mean "Paris, Texas" without writing out "Paris, Texas" are few), we determine the appropriate referent through a combination of heuristics (where and when the book was published, the nations containing the greatest number of its other named locations) and hand review.[26]

Finally, we review by hand the places that occur most frequently in the corpus. That is, for every place name that occurs, on average, at least once every 5 million words (the equivalent of about once in every fifty volumes), we examine the location to which that place name is mapped, correcting the mapping globally or by volume where appropriate. Where relevant and practicable, we map historical places ("Soviet Union," "Smyrna") to their nearest modern equivalent ("Russia," "İzmir"). By focusing on the most frequently occurring locations (about 1% of unique place names), we are able to review 70% of the total location occurrences in the corpus.

Machine learning researchers use a metric called F_1 to assess the performance of information retrieval systems like ours. F_1 balances two desired features: we want our system to identify all the places used in our corpus (that is, it should have high recall) and we want all the places we identify to be correct (it should have high precision). F_1 is the harmonic mean of precision and recall. In our case, precision is 89.7%, recall is 71.0%, and F1 is 79.3%; we miss some locations, but the locations we do identify are generally correct. In many of the instances we care about, a more forgiving metric is appropriate, one that asks only if we have correctly identified the primary national or subnational (state, province, etc.) setting of a book by the preponderance of identified location references. We get the primary national setting right 96% of the time and the primary top-level subnational setting right 92% of the time.

---

[26] Here, too, there are opportunities for improvement through neural language models, though we are not aware of any currently existing, publicly available model that has been trained or evaluated for the task, and the set of importantly ambiguous locations is smaller than one might imagine.

On the whole, our pipeline performs well, though it is far from perfect. It is well suited to the comparative analysis of similarly constituted corpora and subcorpora. In these cases, the phenomena of interest are typically relative differences or rates of change that are robust to baseline errors, and the errors in any one volume can be offset in others. This statistical approach to robustness and error isn't yet typical in literary-historical work, but it is the foundation of not just the physical sciences but the contemporary social sciences as well. We hope to show, in the sections ahead, that it is equally appropriate in cases that interest humanists.

4 Measuring Spatial Mobility

Few would dispute that, as a group, women in Britain have historically been less geographically mobile than men. Biological and social connections to childbirth and childrearing tended to root women of reproductive age, while fewer opportunities for education, employment, and adventure for women of all ages limited their horizons. Most readers would expect to see that difference in geographic mobility reflected in literary texts. Literature, after all, is often used as evidence of historical experience and, secondarily, is often regarded as an influence on extra-literary experience.

But the historical contours of that gendered difference in mobility are harder to pin down. For example, it seems self-evident that the discrepancy between men and women's geographic range in both life and literature diminished between 1800 and 2009 as women closed a range of opportunity gaps. But was this a steady, linear change or a development characterized by rapid shifts and periods of stability (or even of retrenchment)? How might our corpus of more than 20,000 works of fiction provide (or fail to provide) evidence of a change in men and women's geographical range, at least in the realm of the imagination? How, in other words, can we measure men and women's comparative geographic mobility, as represented in literary texts?

In this section we discuss two proxies among many for geographic mobility: attention to international locations and spatial range. Since we are studying British fiction, we can summarize the former simply as the fraction of named locations that are outside the UK's (present-day) borders. How much of a book's geographic imagination is given to national cities, streets, and landmarks, and how much is directed at other nations and the places within them? Spatial range refers to the distance between named locations. A book set entirely in Greece, for example, would register as highly international but with little spatial range. We assess how men and women authors and their gendered characters compare on these two metrics, describe the process by which we derived these conclusions, and consider the implications of our findings for gender-based analysis of fictional texts.

4.1 International Attention

We find that, as expected, male authors name more international locations as a fraction of all locations mentioned than do women. This is the case in the cumulative 209 years of our study and it is also the case in both the nineteenth and the twentieth centuries, considered independently. But the difference is surprisingly modest. Cumulatively, named locations in books by men were about 68% international, while those by women were about 64% international, a difference of just 4 percentage points.[27] In some five-year intervals, the difference between the internationalism of men and women authors was reversed or was too small to be statistically significant; that is, there are brief periods during which we can't be sure there was a difference at all.

The difference between men and women authors' international attention was greatest in the second half of the nineteenth century (especially the 1850s, 1860s, and 1870s) and the second half of the twentieth century (especially the 1950s, 1960s, and 1970s). In the first half of both centuries, there was no statistically significant gap in international attention between texts by men and those by women.

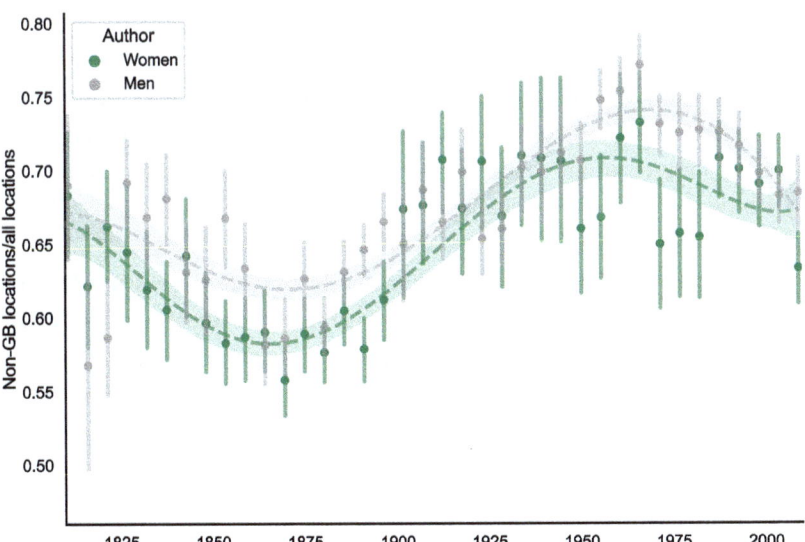

Figure 2 International attention by author gender over time.

---

[27] $p = 3.0 \times 10^{-28}$. All findings are significant at the $p \leq 0.05$ (generally, as here, much less) level unless otherwise noted. p values indicate the probability of encountering under a null hypothesis a result as extreme or more extreme than the one observed. More colloquially, they measure the probability that the observed result is due to chance, given what we know about the variability of the data. Smaller p values indicate greater confidence that the observed result reflects a real difference between the two groups.

> **HOW TO READ THE GRAPHS**
>
> The *y* **(vertical) axis** corresponds to a dependent variable of interest, which is always labeled vertically along the axis itself. In Figure 2, the *y* axis shows the fraction of all named locations that were outside the (present-day) UK. The *x* **(horizontal) axis** corresponds to a different, independent variable, generally historical time as captured by the publication date of the books in the corpus.
>
> Each **dot** on the graph is the mean (average) value of the dependent variable as measured in all books published in a five-year bin. So, in Figure 2, each dot tells us the mean fraction of international locations in books published over five-year periods between 1810 and 2009 by men and by women. While the data we report and analyze begins with books published in 1800, we trim our figures at 1810 to avoid occasional visual artifacts that result from small samples in the earliest years. The **vertical bar** surrounding each dot is the 95% confidence interval for that mean. Longer bars indicate greater uncertainty of the mean, typically because the individual values are either widely dispersed or because there aren't very many of them.
>
> The **line** moving horizontally through time is the line of best fit (calculated using a fifth-order polynomial) through the data, with **shading** to show the 95% confidence interval of the fit. As with the vertical error bars, wider shaded regions indicate greater uncertainty concerning the exact location of the line of best fit. The line of best fit helps us to see trends across the two centuries, while the dots give us more detail in narrower time frames.
>
> **Colors and textures:** Throughout the text, figures representing data aggregated by *author* gender (as in Figure 2) use green markers and dashed fit lines. Figures that show *character* gender use purple markers and solid fit lines. Figures that are not aggregated by gender use blue markers.

A more interesting finding may be just how *large* the international fractions were. Roughly two thirds of all geographic references were to places beyond British borders. A comparable study of American fiction over the same period found roughly 35%–40% of named locations were international in the US case (Wilkens, "Too Isolated").

The fluctuations across the period are interesting, too. As we might expect, fiction of the early twentieth century – an era associated with cosmopolitan

Gender and Literary Geography 27

modernism and with two world wars – was more international (about 15% more) than was fiction of the late nineteenth century. However, this rise was partly making up ground lost from the fifty years before. Counterintuitively, the second half of the nineteenth century – when the British Empire was expanding – was a period of relative insularity (as measured by geographic references) in British fiction, though the fraction of international attention was still notably high in comparison with the American case (which was also much more stable over historical time). Critics have sometimes noted a potential suppression of direct engagement with the sites of empire during the height of colonial expansion, offering a range of possible explanations. Fredric Jameson, for one, has argued that, before World War I, "the relationship of domination between First and Third World was masked and displaced by an overriding (and perhaps ideological) consciousness of imperialism as being essentially a relationship between First World powers or the holders of Empire, and this consciousness tended to repress the more basic axis of otherness, and to raise issues of colonial reality only incidentally" ("Modernism and Imperialism"). And we have seen, in other contexts, that, even in the absence of explicit ideological suppression, certain types of geographical attention evolve only slowly, over decades or generations (Wilkens, "Literary Attention Lag"). Here, we offer the first large-scale evidence that, relatively speaking, British fiction did indeed engage more intensively with colonial and other extraterritorial locations in the twentieth century than during the nineteenth. There are other ways to assess international investments, of course; we will consider them in the sections ahead.

Table 1 lists some relatively well-known books that were close to the period average, far below it, and far above it, in the fraction of their locations allocated internationally. A few patterns quickly emerge. Unsurprisingly, the least international books take place entirely in the UK, often in circumscribed settings. These need not be rural settings, however: Margaret Oliphant's *A House in Bloomsbury* and G. K. Chesterton's *The Napoleon of Notting Hill*, for example, take place in particular neighborhoods of London (named in their very titles). As importantly, their imaginative universe is also local, with few references to foreign locations. In contrast, the most international books are set outside of the UK and include translated works by foreign writers (such as André Gide, *Prometheus Illbound*) and stories gathered from elsewhere (as with Mary Agnes Hamilton's *Greek Legends*).

The works closer to average in their international fraction are perhaps more enlightening. Their major settings include the UK, but they are not exclusively set there. Elizabeth von Arnim's *The Enchanted April* (1922), for

Table 1 Sample texts in each of four half-century periods that were far below average, about average, and far above average (for the period) in the fraction of named locations outside the UK.

Period	Least international	Near average international	Most international
1800–1850	Elizabeth Gaskell, *Mary Barton* Caroline Lamb, *Graham Hamilton*	Regina Maria Roche, *The Bridal of Dunamore* Frederick Marryat, *The King's Own*	Edward Bulwer Lytton, *Rienzi* Benjamin Disraeli, *The Wondrous Tale of Alroy*
1851–1900	Margaret Oliphant, *A House in Bloomsbury* Wilkie Collins, *The Woman in White*	E. Lynn Linton, *With a Silken Thread* George Moore, *Confessions of a Young Man*	Charles Kingsley, *Hypatia* George Eliot, *Romola*
1901–1950	Virginia Woolf, *Night and Day* G. K. Chesterton, *The Napoleon of Notting Hill*	Elizabeth von Arnim, *The Enchanted April* Aldous Huxley, *Brief Candles*	Mary Agnes Hamilton, *Greek Legends* C. A. Kincaid, *An Anthology of Indian Tales*
1951–2009	Peter Ackroyd, *Chatterton* Hilary Mantel, *Beyond Black*	Samuel Selvon, *Moses Migrating*	Salman Rushdie, *Midnight's Children*

example, has two settings: its early pages are set in London, while most of the remainder of the novel takes place in rural Italy. Though the majority of the narrative is set in Italy, the London portions are geographically intense, which explains why the book isn't more international than around the period average of 70%. The lower, but still significant, average degree of internationalism in books of the late nineteenth century – 61% international – is well illustrated by George Moore's *Confessions of a Young Man* (1888), which is set in Paris and London.

While author gender played only an apparently modest role in books' degree of internationalism, differences in international geographic attention by gender were more pronounced when our unit of measurement is the poles of gendered character space.[28] Books mostly about men were distinctly more international in their location usage than were books mostly about women – about 20% more across the full corpus.[29] In terms of gendered character space, the gap between masculine and feminine international attention remained relatively consistent across the centuries of our study, as shown in Figure 3.

While conforming to prior expectations about men's greater mobility, the results probably also reflect gendered literary genres and gendered character roles. Seafaring yarns and adventure tales tend to have predominantly male characters; characters with positions in government or international business have been more likely to be men from 1800 onward. But we know very little about the large-scale evolution of genres over the last two centuries, so it is difficult to disentangle shifts *between* genres that use men and women

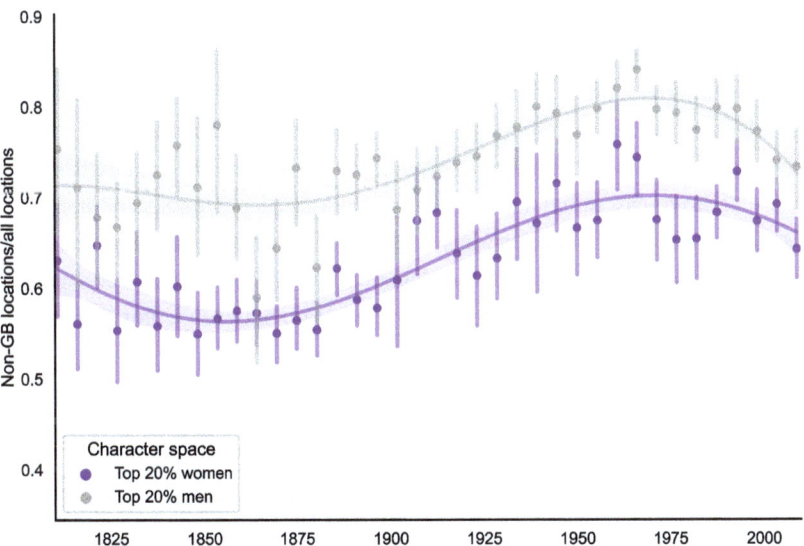

Figure 3 Books that are mostly about men have a higher average fraction of named locations outside the UK than do books mostly about women.

---

[28] We say "apparently" modest because, throughout the period, men and women authors wrote more about characters of their own gender than of other genders (see Underwood et al.). While author gender and the gendered poles of character space are often intersectional, we consider them separately here. We treat their intersection later in this section and elsewhere in the Element.

[29] Reporting differences in percentage values is always tricky. Here, we calculate the difference between the average international location fraction in books about men (0.7568), subtract the average international fraction in books about women (0.6340), and divide by the same international fraction in books about women (as our baseline). The calculation is (0.7568–0.6340)/0.6340 = 19.4%.

characters at different rates from changes in gender usage *within* genres over time. If the generic distribution of the HathiTrust corpus becomes better known in the future, we could directly disambiguate the findings to determine how much of the difference we see in gendered characters' international links is the result of genre choices (spy fiction versus domestic romance novels, say) and how much difference occurs within the same genre. That said, the choice to write in a particular genre is also a choice about whether the story will likely contain more men or women. As Mikhail Bakhtin argued decades ago – and as Franco Moretti has more recently re-emphasized – *where* a book is set determines *what* will happen (Bakhtin, *Dialogic*; Moretti, *Graphs*, ch. 3). We would add that setting also determines to *whom* events will happen. If women-centered genres rise in popularity, that fact would signal a preference for a certain form of geographic attention, and vice versa, even in the absence of intra-generic geographic change.

Intriguingly, women authors created greater difference between character genders than did men (Figure 4). In sum, women's gender-skewed texts were more different (at 14.5 percentage points) in their international attention than were analogously imbalanced texts by men (at 9.5 percentage points). That is, the women-authored case has a nearly 50% greater gap than the male-authored one. The effect is that readers of books by women have consistently encountered larger gaps in international attention between women-heavy and men-heavy books than have readers of books by men. Whether women authors have been more conservative or more realistic, this pattern remained true across each fifty-year period, though the exact degree of difference fluctuated slightly, with the greatest variance in the earliest years of our study.[30] We flag this result specifically as meriting further investigation, since it conforms to no existing theory of gendered authorship of which we are aware.

The degree of international attention (as a fraction of all geographic attention), then, is one way to compare mobility. We've compared by author gender, by gendered character space in the most single-gender-dominant texts, and by men and women authors' own differentiation in single-gender-dominant texts. We've seen that, although male authors' degree of attention to international locations was only modestly greater than that of women authors, both categories

---

[30] Note that the absolute magnitude of the gap in international attention between books about men and books about women declined during the twentieth century (as shown by the downward slope of the fit lines in Figure 4), but the magnitude of the *difference* between the gap in texts by women and texts by men (the distance between the two fit lines at any given date) shows very little change over time after about 1900.

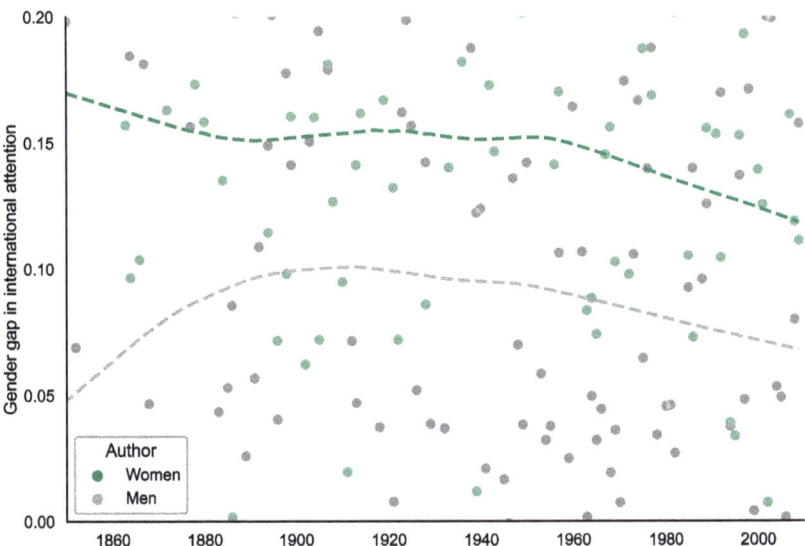

Figure 4 Women authors allocate international space more differently between books about women and those about men than do male authors. We plot the difference (gap) in the annual raw fraction of international locations used in gender-skewed texts by women (green) and by men (black). Trend line is a LOESS estimate. Note that the horizontal axis begins at 1850; data are too sparse for useful comparison in the early decades of the nineteenth century.

of authors, but especially women, were decisive in associating international locations more with male characters.

Before we move on to further analysis of gender's role in geographic attention, we should consider a more fine-grained problem: how the fraction of references to *particular* international locations changed over time – and how they didn't. (We'll also consider a different approach to this question, built around the average *specificity* of geographic references, in Section 5.) Table 2 shows the top international locations in each half century, as well as the most frequently occurring locations (of any type) in the corpus as a whole.[31] Paris and France were the most frequently referenced locations beyond the UK's borders in every period, providing a measure of quantitative support for Pascale Casanova's argument in *The World Republic of Letters* that Paris was the center of the (imagined) literary world. Ireland was prominent in early nineteenth-century British fiction, but

---

[31] We do not discuss in this study the most frequent locations (domestic and international) in the corpus as a whole, finding them similar to those observed in previous work (Evans and Wilkens; Wilkens, "Too Isolated"; Wilkens et al.). We do note that "London" and "England" are exceedingly common in the corpus, occurring about two to three times more often than any other single location.

Table 2 Top international locations by era and, for reference, top overall locations in the full corpus (shaded cells in rightmost column).

Rank	1800–1850	1851–1900	1901–1950	1951–2009	All locations, all years (per 100 k words)
1.	Paris	Paris	Paris	Paris	London (18.3)
2.	France	France	France	France	England (11.7)
3.	Ireland	India	India	America	Paris (6.7)
4.	Rome	Rome	Russia	New York	France (5.0)
5.	Italy	Italy	Europe	Europe	India (2.8)
6.	Spain	Europe	Rome	Africa	Europe (2.7)
7.	Europe	Ireland	Germany	India	Rome (2.6)
8.	Naples	America	America	Rome	America (2.5)
9.	Dublin	Sydney	Ireland	Germany	Ireland (2.4)
10.	India	New York	New York	Italy	Italy (2.3)

diminishingly so in the decades and centuries that followed.[32] Rome and Italy were named more in the nineteenth century than in the twentieth, when their use declined. By the late nineteenth century, India rose in the ranks and would stay in the third position until after its independence. Africa, on the other hand, didn't enter the top 10 until most of its colonized nations were achieving independence. Russia and Germany rose in the era of the world wars. Russia was the object of particular attention, probably boosted by widespread interest in – and concern about – the Russian Revolution, socialism, and communism. America and its most famous city rose in prominence as the centuries progressed. In sum, Western Europe was important in British literature throughout the nineteenth and twentieth centuries, part of a preference for the near over the far. In contrast, the empire's colonies make little appearance in the most frequently named places, Ireland and India being notable exceptions.

4.2 Geographic Range

Internationalism is an important aspect of literary-geographic mobility. But it's not the only one. Another approach to measuring imaginative mobility is to consider books' spatial *range*, regardless of national boundaries. In this case, we seek to measure the geographic extent of each book. It's a tricky metric to formulate; we want to account for large distances without being unduly

---

[32] For more on the status of Ireland as an "international" and colonial location in British fiction, see Evans and Wilkens, "Nation" and influential scholarship including Kiberd, *Inventing Ireland*.

influenced by fleeting mentions of far-off locales, and we want (all else being equal) to rank highly geographically diverse books above those that focus on a few widely separated places.

To calculate the geographic range of each book, we first restricted the locations under consideration to those that were among the 1,200 most frequently occurring in the corpus as a whole (to keep the total set of location pairs manageable). We then calculated the distance between every possible pair of these high-frequency places in a given text, scaled the distance between them according to their relative frequency in the volume, and weighted each pair by the fraction of all volume-level occurrences represented by members of the pair.

Scaling has the effect of reducing the calculated distance between two locations when one is used more often than the other. Weighting ensures that the range of a book is not inflated simply because a book is geographically intensive (we aim to avoid calculating a large range for a book in which there are many references to different parts of a single city versus one in which there are fewer but more widely dispersed locations). We designed this metric to capture absolute geographic extent, but also to differentiate books that focus on a small area while mentioning a few distant locations from those that spread their geographic attention more equally over large distances.

A handful of examples may help to clarify the somewhat complicated range metric. A book that mentions London once, Paris once, and Berlin once has a calculated geographic range of 2,158 kilometers, which is simply the sum of the pairwise distances between those three cities. Substituting Melbourne for Berlin raises the range to 34,029 km, since Melbourne is over 16,000 km from London and from Paris. A book that mentions London ten times and Melbourne once, however, has a geographic range of only 3,072 km, since the distance from London to Melbourne (16,899 km) is scaled downward by a factor of 2/11 (two times the relative frequency of the less-used city; here 2 * 1/11) to account for the much greater relative usage of London. The last example exaggerates the scaling effect by imagining a book that uses only two locations, but the idea is clear: our range calculation treats this hypothetical volume as one that's mostly about a single city (but not exclusively so; its range is 50% greater than the London-Paris-Berlin example). There is room for debate about the suitability of the metric as we have designed it, but we believe that it captures much of our readerly sense of geographic range in the absence of the ability to reliably parse temporally ordered journeys by individual characters.[33]

---

[33] See the online supplementary materials for full details. For recent work that assesses mobility by tracking individual characters through geonarrative space, see Soni et al., "Grounding"; and Wilkens et al., "Small Worlds."

We discovered that books by male authors showed consistently greater spatial range than did those by women authors (despite their quite similar international usage rates), and that spatial range increased for both categories of writers over the centuries (Figure 5(a)). There were times, however, of relative stability in the degree of spatial range (the early twentieth century) and times of rapid increase (the late twentieth century). Remember that characters did not necessarily travel more or farther (although they probably did); the data shows us all named places, in a variety of contexts, including descriptive asides, such as "carpets from Turkey" and "politics in Australia," as well as indications of setting. Nonetheless, the imaginative map of the literary world expanded at a relatively steady rate between the early nineteenth century and the late twentieth, so that the average book today has about three times the geographic range as did one published two centuries ago.

The case of gendered character-space was more complex (Figure 5(b)). Books devoted mostly to women characters increased steadily in their geographic range across the entire period, with the notable exceptions of the leveling off that we've already observed in the early twentieth century and a more rapid increase in the late twentieth century. The geographic range of male-dominated books took a different course, with the last decades of the nineteenth century evincing greater spatial range than the next seventy-plus years. A curious paradox emerges in books mostly about men: their geographic range increases in the late nineteenth century and drops in the early twentieth century, even as the opposite occurs in their fraction of named locations that are international. The influence of World War I provides one possible explanation: references to the main theaters of war in Western Europe may have entailed an increase in international references even as geographic range shrank on a global scale, far away places like Australia and Canada becoming of less interest than locations in France and Belgium. Meanwhile, women in fiction were traveling farther as the decades progressed, even while the places to which they traveled remained slightly more limited to locations within the nation.

✷✷✷

In conclusion, some critical assumptions about the role of gender in geographic mobility are confirmed by our quantitative findings. Geographic references associated with male authors and characters were more international and showed greater spatial range than did geographic references associated with women authors and characters. Several interesting discoveries, however, provide valuable nuance to these broad patterns. First, the *differences* between men's and women's mobility, whether measured by author gender or character space, changed little over the 209 years of our study. Of the four measurements

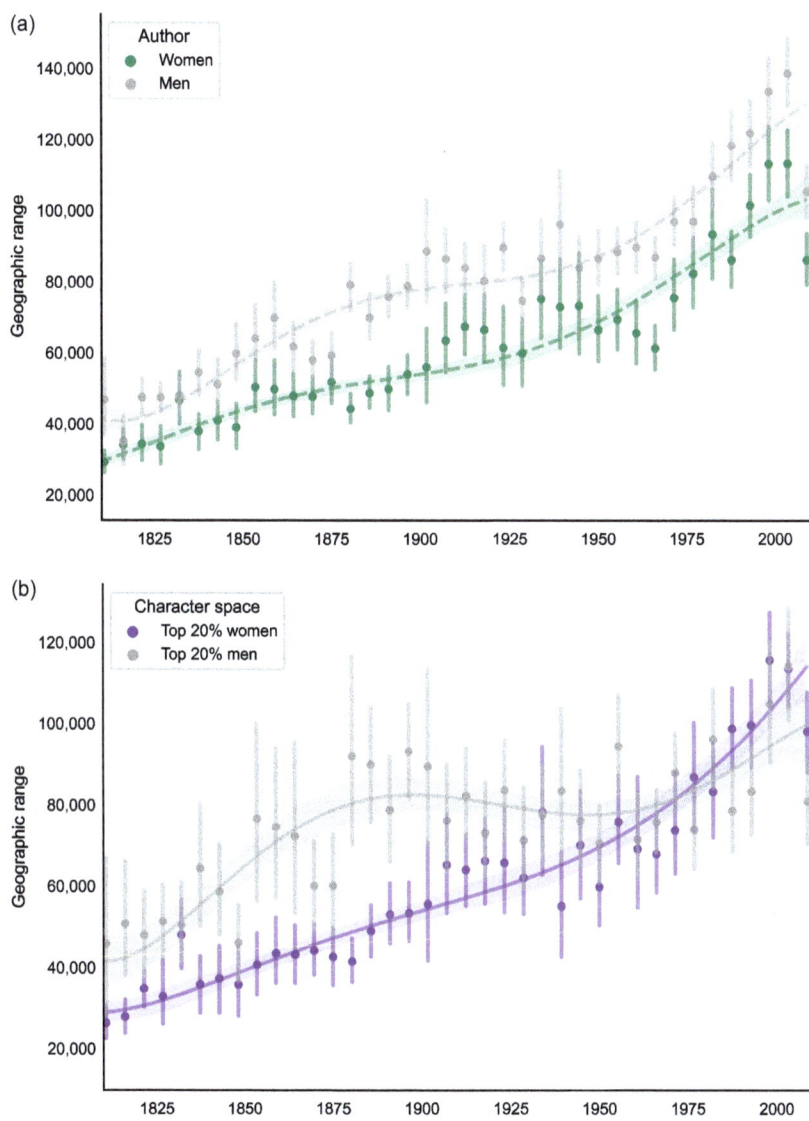

Figure 5 Geographic range over time by (a) author gender and (b) character gender.

we discuss in detail, only one case showed women catching up with and perhaps surpassing men in terms of mobility (this case was in the last fifty years of geographic range). Otherwise, by our metrics, male writers and male characters remained consistently more mobile than women writers and characters. Like Underwood, Bamman, and Lee's discovery about the shocking durability of some aspects of gender representation, our findings demonstrate how ensconced are spatial relationships in the construction of gender.

Second, without regard to gender, time *was* a significant factor in rates of international references and in spatial range. Some changes over time, such as the increasing spatial range of geographic references, are compatible with the widespread sense of what it means to live in an increasingly globalized world. We have ceased to be surprised that Bangalore, Shenzhen, and Los Angeles may all be nodes on a single supply chain, even as global tourism has become widely available to the middle-classes and refugees have been displaced around the world. It makes sense that British fiction would reflect a world that is, in significant ways, more densely interconnected. A turn outward is reflected, too, though more modestly, in the degree of attention to international locations.

Finally, we found that *character* gender is (and has long been) a stronger predictor of geographic mobility than is *author* gender. The relatively slight difference between men and women authors in their international attention, for example, becomes a pronounced difference between books that are mostly about men and those that are mostly about women. This finding calls for caution in linking literary depictions with historical experience, a tactic common in both literary and historical research. We can, in a sense, measure the distance between history and literature in the gendered differences between authorial options and character environments. One explanation for this is to say that fiction exaggerates for effect what authors observe in real life. It may be that the separation of the spheres was greater in books than it was in the world, even as real differences in men's and women's mobility have been remarkably and disturbingly consistent over two centuries of purported progress.

5 Geographic Intensity and Specificity

In the previous section, we used two measures – international attention and geographic range – to help us assess spatial mobility in literary texts. We found that, while masculinity has typically been associated with greater attention to locations outside Britain and with more widely dispersed literary settings – and while these gendered associations have changed less than we might have expected between the early nineteenth century and today – both forms of geographic investment evolved significantly and in surprising ways over time. We found, for example, quite a bit of nonlinear development, including cases where multiple decades of evolution toward greater or lesser mobility were followed by marked swings back toward older norms.

We turn now to a different aspect of literary geography. In this section, we are concerned with the degree and the types of literary-geographic investment. In other words, where the last section examined measures of spatial *distribution*, the present one involves matters of spatial *depth* or detail. If British literature became more widely distributed – more international and more diverse – over time, did it necessarily also become more geographically intensive, devoting more narrative space to naming and examining the geographic world? Did those changes in intensity, if any, take the form of greater attention to the texture and details of place, to streets, buildings, houses, neighborhoods, monuments, and the like? Or (and both could be true, for reasons we explore in the conclusion to this section), did books more often eschew such fine-grained elements of setting in favor of the high-level spaces of nations and regions, perhaps because those books involved more often political and economic themes that were best framed in abstract rather than specific geographic terms?

There are reasons, of course, to think that geographic depth may not behave in the same ways as does spatial distribution. Imagine a narrative model with two poles. One possibility is that books with limited geographic diversity or range (which are disproportionately books by and about women) *concentrate* their geographic investments. In that case, we would expect those books to show the same level of total geographic usage but, because their attention is spread over smaller areas, to be in general more specific or detailed in their spatial descriptions. They might prefer, for instance, to name individual buildings and streets rather than cities or nations. We might call this the specificity pole. Alternatively, books that cover less ground might be no more specific about the ground they do cover, implying that those books are simply less geographically intensive, given their more prescribed spatial bounds. We could call this the curtailment pole. The actual case probably lies somewhere between the two.

We also want to know how these aspects of geographic depth have been treated in British literature and how the books in our corpus have navigated the spectrum of specificity and constraint. We are especially eager to measure and characterize the interplay of gendered responses to women's lower mobility, as well as the historical development of those differences. Much depends on the answers to all of these questions, since they can help us understand both the literary effects of gender discrimination (now and in the past) and, even more generally, the ways in which literature responds to cultural constraints.

5.1 Methods

We work with the same corpus of 21,347 books and the same set of extracted geographic data that we described in Sections 2 and 3, and that we used in Section 4. We now introduce three basic measures of geographic depth derived from this data.

The first measure, *intensity*, is the simplest: it is the total number of location occurrences per 100,000 words in each volume. We want to draw attention to the fact that normalizing by length at the volume level in this way means that each book contributes equal weight to our aggregated measures; as is true elsewhere in the study, long books are neither more nor less important than short books in our model. This is an interpretive choice, one that treats books themselves (rather than authors or periods, for example) as the basic units of our analysis.

In addition to intensity, we calculate two different measures of geographic specificity, which together allow us to assess the granularity of spatial attention in each book. Our first specificity measure, *subcountry specificity*, is the fraction of locations for a given nation or global region that are more specific (equivalently, that represent lower-level political entities) than the nation itself. The second measure, *subcity specificity*, is analogous, but measures the (smaller) fraction of locations for a given nation or region that correspond to areas below the city level (neighborhoods, streets, parks, and the like).

We'll have more to say about how we interpret these metrics as we review our results. For the moment, we note that subcity specificity serves as a proxy for setting-level details, that is, for the geographic component of characters' and communities' daily lives. Subcountry specificity consolidates aspects of the text that generally do not involve international attention (which is most likely to be expressed at the level of nations and supranational regions) but may include national and subnational affairs. So, where intensity measures the overall depth of a book's geographic investment, our specificity metrics help us characterize the nature of that depth.

One last detail. We have calculated two versions of our UK subcountry specificity metric, one that treats England, Scotland, Wales, and Northern Ireland as the administrative subunits of the UK that they officially are, the other that reflects common usage and treats the Home Nations as the equivalent of countries (hence excluding references to them from the count of specific subcountry-level entities). The Home-Nations-as-countries version is generally preferred, since it avoids the misleading appearance of much lower specificity that otherwise results from the sociolinguistic shift toward "Britain" from "England" as the preferred national reference in the twentieth century. In every case, we treat "Britain" and "Great Britain" as synonyms for the United Kingdom (of Great Britain and Northern Ireland). In keeping with our global practice, we exclude Ireland and other former British colonies from our counts of British locations at all times, regardless of their status at the time of publication of any book in our corpus.

5.2 Intensity

We begin with geographic intensity, our simple measure of the rate at which a book mentions geographic locations. Books that are most geographically intense often focus on a single place named in the very title, such as Charles Sedley's *A Winter in Dublin* (1808) and Yoshio Markino's *A Japanese Artist in London* (1910). The least geographically intense typically involve fantasy or a removal from the ordinary world, as with Ford Madox Ford's *The Queen Who Flew* (1894), William Golding's *Lord of the Flies* (1955), and Ben Okri's *Starbook: A Magical Tale of Love and Regeneration* (2007). Books that are near average in geographic intensity, which include Frederick Denison Maurice's *Eustace Conway* (1834), E. M. Forster's *The Longest Journey* (1907), and Nadine Gordimer's *Crimes of Conscience* (1991), include a range of subgenres but are generally realist.

We find that books by men were on average about 20% more intense in their geographic references than were books by women. And while the intensity of male authors' geographic references held fairly steady over time, women authors' geographic intensity dipped in the late nineteenth century, rose in the early twentieth century, and partly receded in the late twentieth (Figure 6).

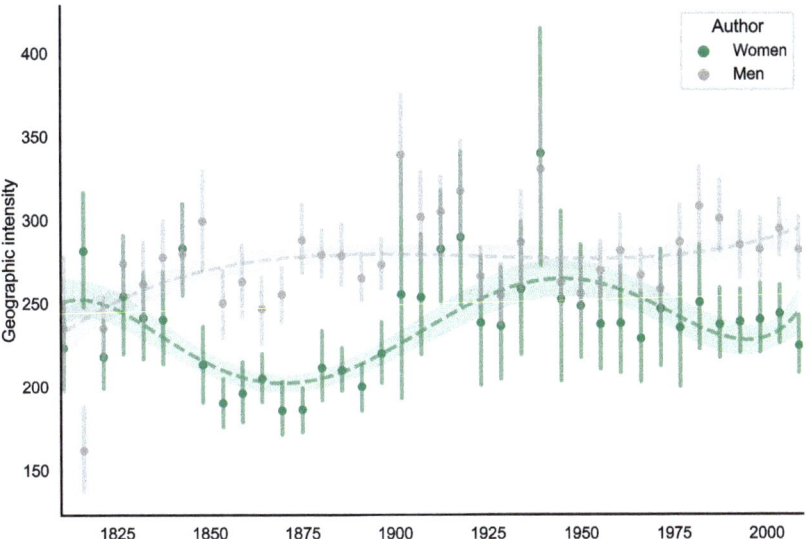

Figure 6 Geographic intensity in books by men and by women. The vertical axis indicates the number of words out of 100,000 that are geographic locations.

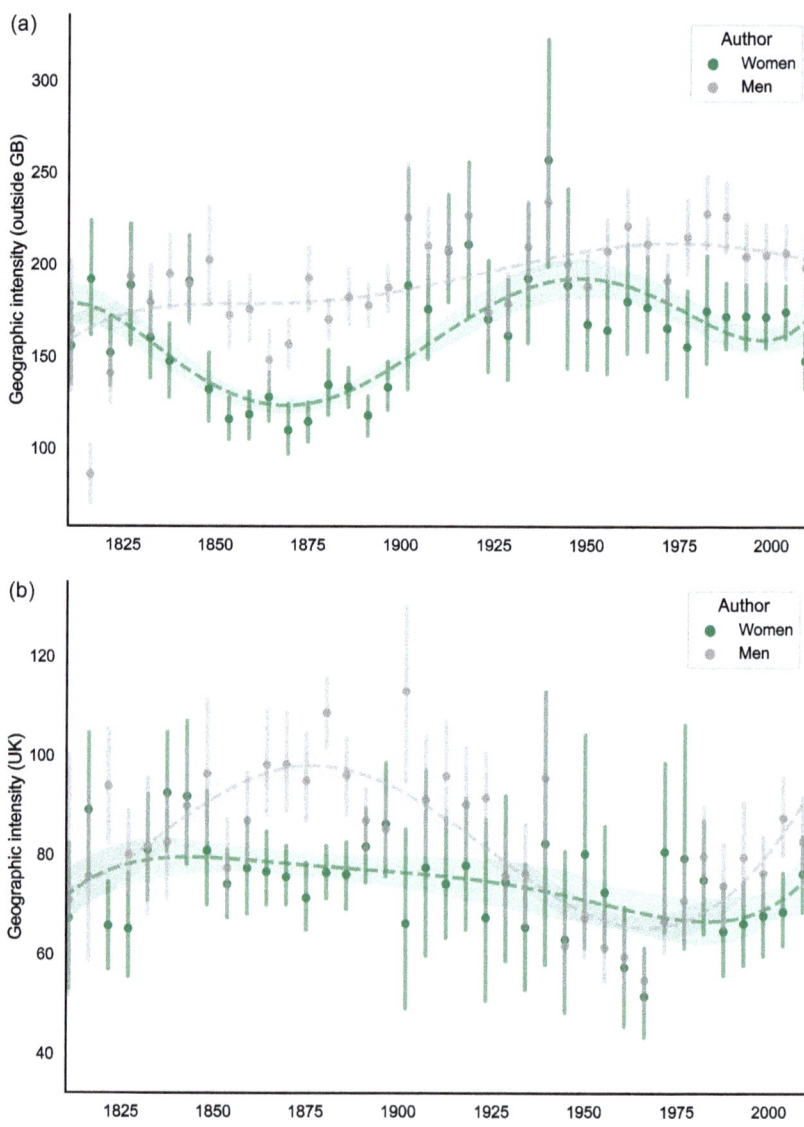

Figure 7 Authors' geographic intensity (a) outside the UK and (b) within the UK.

It is tempting to explain the first part of this trend through the ascendance of separate sphere ideology in the Victorian period (discussed in more detail in Section 6). The late nineteenth-century dip, however, was really a phenomenon outside the UK, as we see when we distinguish domestic from international intensity (Figure 7). Within the UK, women writers' intensity is relatively steady in the period, while male authors increased their intensity in the late nineteenth century, decreased it in the mid twentieth century, and increased again in the late twentieth century. One possible explanation for the rise in the nineteenth century is the advent of railway travel and, consequently, the rapid increase in the circulation of goods and people within the UK (Bogart et al.; Mullen). While men and women were both impacted by these developments, the effects were likely greater for men, whose mobility was rarely challenged. The reduction of national geographic intensity, especially in books by men, in the mid-twentieth century is largely explained by their turn to international locations following the outbreak of the second world war and, post-war, by colonial independence movements and increased global trade. (See Section 4 for a discussion of the changing fraction of attention devoted to international sites.) After around 1875, UK intensity in books by men (shown in Figure 7(b)) looks similar to the inverse of men's international fraction in Figure 2.)

Comparing geographic intensity in books grouped by dominant character gender reveals similar trends over time (Figure 8). Books that devoted most of their character space to men were again more steadily geographically intense throughout the period than were books that devoted most of their space to women. Women-heavy books again decreased in intensity in the nineteenth century, then rose in the early twentieth century. The difference between genders was significantly greater in character space than among authors, a pattern we have seen across many metrics. Here, books with character space dominated by men were about a third more geographically intense overall than

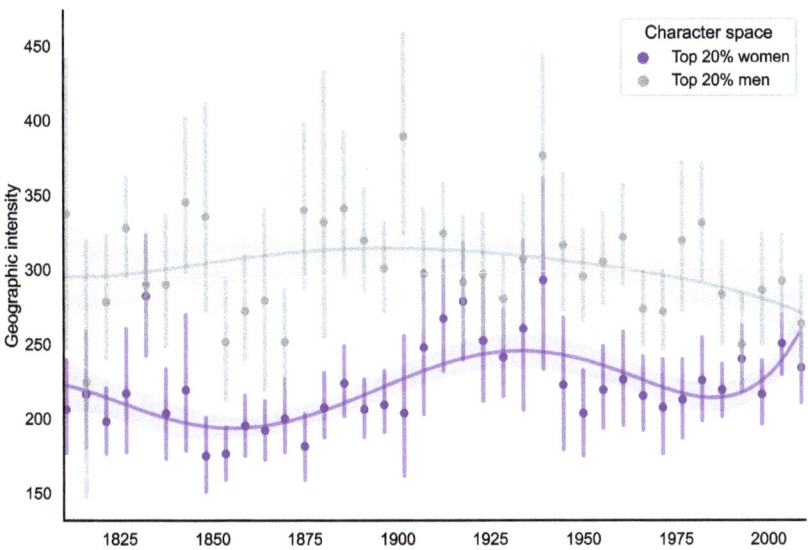

Figure 8 Geographic intensity of gendered character space.

those skewed toward women (compared to about 20% in the case of men versus women authors).

Trends within and beyond the UK resembled those observed in the case of author genders: large differences outside the UK, much smaller gaps within it. The greater intensity of locations within the nation, compared to without, of feminine character space suggests the effects of limited international travel on conceptions of where British women could be imagined believably. UK geographic intensity declined over time in books about men and in those about women, but the change was smaller in women-centered books, again likely owing to differences in international attention as men turned increasingly abroad.

Overall, then, we find that the relative intensity of geographic references aligns with existing critical conceptions about the role of gender in writers' and characters' degree of access to locations beyond the home. The majority of the difference lies outside the UK; when it comes to locations within the UK, authors were more similar in their geographic intensity, while books segmented by gendered character space were more similar yet.

Our expectation that gender groups grew closer together over time is supported by these results, but more modestly than we might have hypothesized. We saw that, within the UK, men and women authors did draw closer together in their geographic intensity during the middle decades of the twentieth century, but this was primarily because male writers became less geographically intense within the UK as they became more intense outside of it. Overall, the intensity gap between men and women authors declined only modestly. There was a more significant decrease in gender difference in the case of character space, where the gap closed to a still-sizable 27% from 35% in the earlier century. While books about women were increasingly engaged with geographic locations in the twentieth century, they continued to reference fewer locations than their male-centered counterparts by a significant margin.

5.3 Specificity below the Nation Level

Specificity provides a different way of examining gender's quantitative and qualitative roles in literary geography. When we treat the UK alone as a nation and consider references to England, Wales, Scotland, and Northern Ireland as representing regions below the national level, we find that the UK subnational fraction fell throughout most of the twentieth century for both men and women authors (Figure 9(a)). In the second half of the nineteenth century, about 98% of all domestic locations were below the UK level (e.g., to England and the places within it) whereas 100 years later, about 87% of locations were below the UK

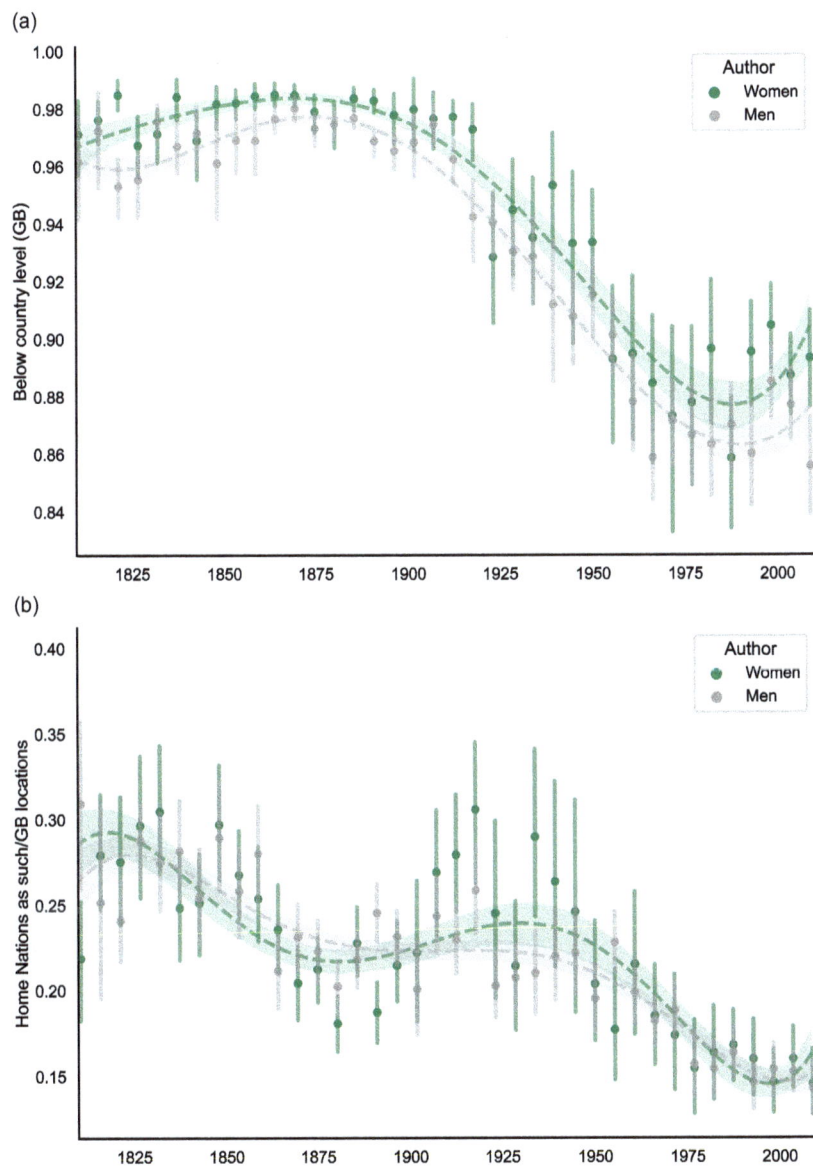

Figure 9 The evolution of specificity in the UK. (a) Geographic specificity below the UK level by author gender. The *y* axis shows the fraction of references to locations within the UK among all references to the UK and to locations within it. (b) The fraction of all references to British locations that name the Home Nations themselves.

level. That is, as time went by, writers devoted more of their attention to the United Kingdom itself, rather than to the places within it. This is in large part a story of linguistic drift, as usage increasingly favored the UK or Great Britain over the Home Nations (see Figure 9(b)). But it also reflects a related underlying historical shift in the idea of the nation itself, as the UK increasingly became the default national unit.

Books mostly about women were also consistently more specific below the UK country level than were their male-oriented counterparts. Both men and women authors made their books about women more specific below the (UK) country level than they did their books centered on men. When we measure the gap in gendered specificity between men and women authors (as opposed to characters), we find a larger difference in the case of books by women. Further, that difference was made up entirely by writers' different treatment of books that devoted most of their character space to women. Authors treated their male characters in similar ways, including associating those characters with the British nation at higher rates over time. But authors diverged in their treatment of women characters, whom women authors associated with greater specificity. As we have seen before, women writers were again more conservative (or realistic) than were their male counterparts regarding changes in their women characters' geographic circumstances.

If we treat the Home Nations as top-level national entities, we observe a larger difference across gendered character space. Books with more character space devoted to women were significantly more specific in their references than were their more masculine counterparts throughout the period (Figure 10; mean difference 12%). When books about women were at their least specific

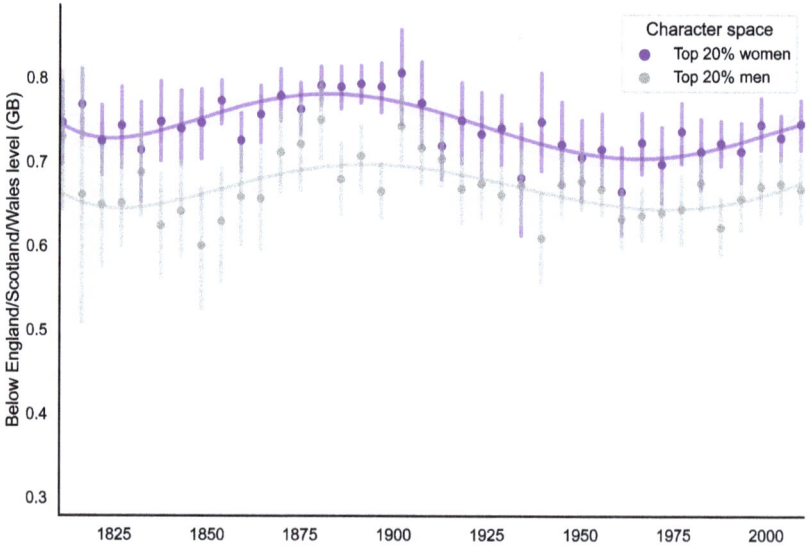

Figure 10 Specificity below Home Nation level by gendered character space.

(in the early 1950s), they were at about the same level – roughly 70% of references below the level of the Home Nations – as were books about men when those books were at their most specific (in the late nineteenth century).

So, while women writers increased their fraction of references to Britain's Home Nations during the period of the world wars (roughly equaling the fraction of attention allocated by male authors), books about women remained persistently more interested in locations at the regional level and below than were books about men. Regardless of which measure of the nation we use, both men and women authors were more specific in books about women than they were in books about men.

Part of the explanation for these differences is male authors' greater treatment of political themes. Political content is strongly correlated with higher geographic intensity and lower specificity (see Figure 11). While we can't infer any necessarily causal relationship in this case, we do have evidence that political books tend to be more geographically invested and that they focus their investment at higher administrative levels.

When referencing locations outside the United Kingdom, authors diminished over time their relative rate of references to subcountry locations, though not with such a dramatic dropoff as with domestic locations. It may be that this change suggests a more politically or nationally oriented view, one in which countries became increasingly more significant than the places within them.

5.4 Specificity below the City Level

The relationship between gender and geographic specificity is different if we look below the level of the city (that is, to particular streets, buildings, squares, and so on) rather than the nation. Male authors were somewhat more specific about locations within the UK through the nineteenth century, while women were very slightly more specific in the last decades of the twentieth century (Figure 12(a)). It's worth noting how low the subcity specificity levels are in general: although subcity specificity rose over time, only about 20% of all named geographical locations occur below the city level. The kinds of highly specific geographic references that many readers associate with books that are invested in a particular place account for only about a fifth of location references. Much more common were references to nations and to cities themselves.

Books mostly about women, however, were more specific below the city level than were books mostly about men during the majority of the twentieth century (Figure 12(b)). When both men and women writers named locations below the city level, that specificity was greatest in both groups' books that devoted most of their character space to women. The difference was especially

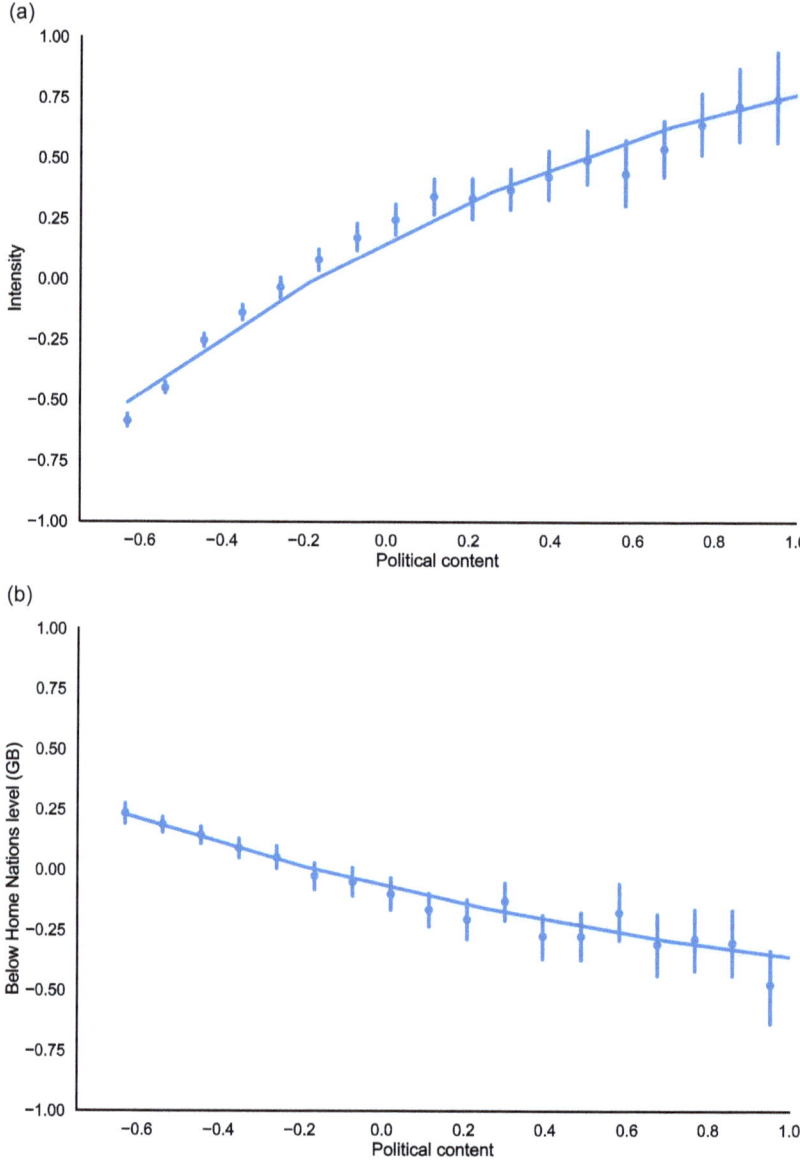

Figure 11 Geographic intensity and specificity as functions of political content. Axes show the number of standard deviations above or below the mean (z-score) for each metric.

strong in the first half of the twentieth century, particularly among women authors, who were nearly 50% more specific below the city level in books about women than in those that were mostly about men. Locations below the

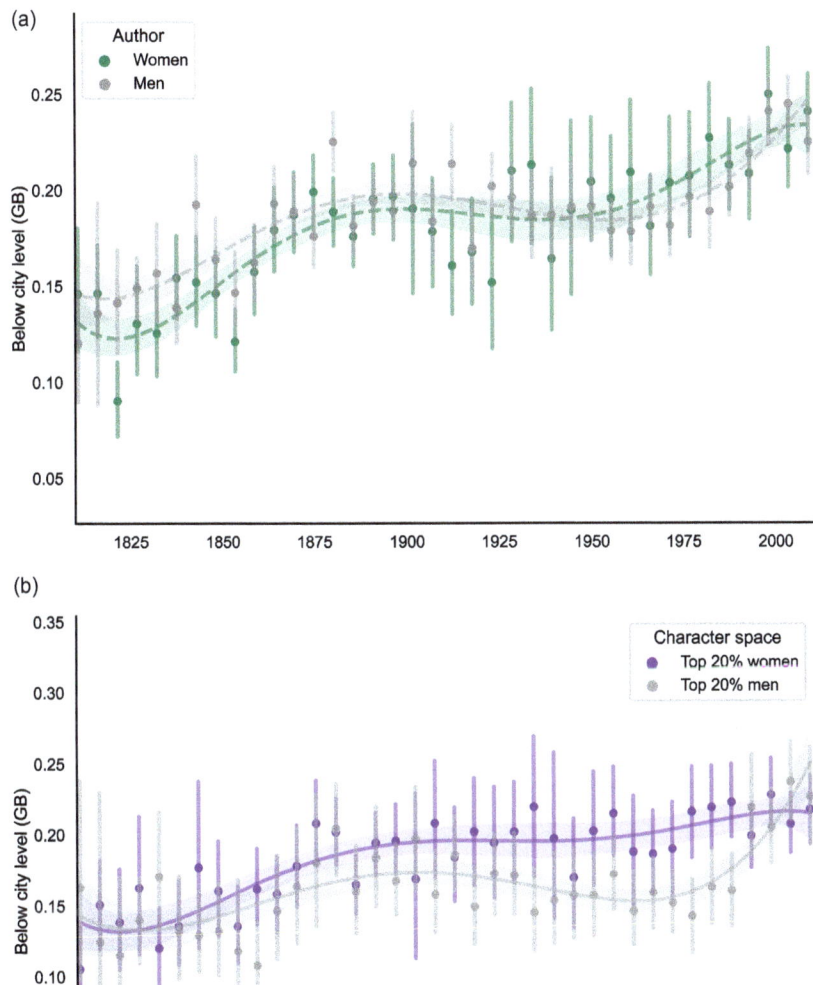

Figure 12 Subcity specificity within the UK by (a) author gender and (b) character gender.

city level are generally present in stories about urban public life. The early twentieth century was a period of increasing urban presence for women, and it seems that women writers were especially keen to represent that fact. In the next section we will consider urban space and its gender associations in depth.

Outside of the UK, women writers were markedly more specific below the city level than were men in the late nineteenth and early twentieth centuries

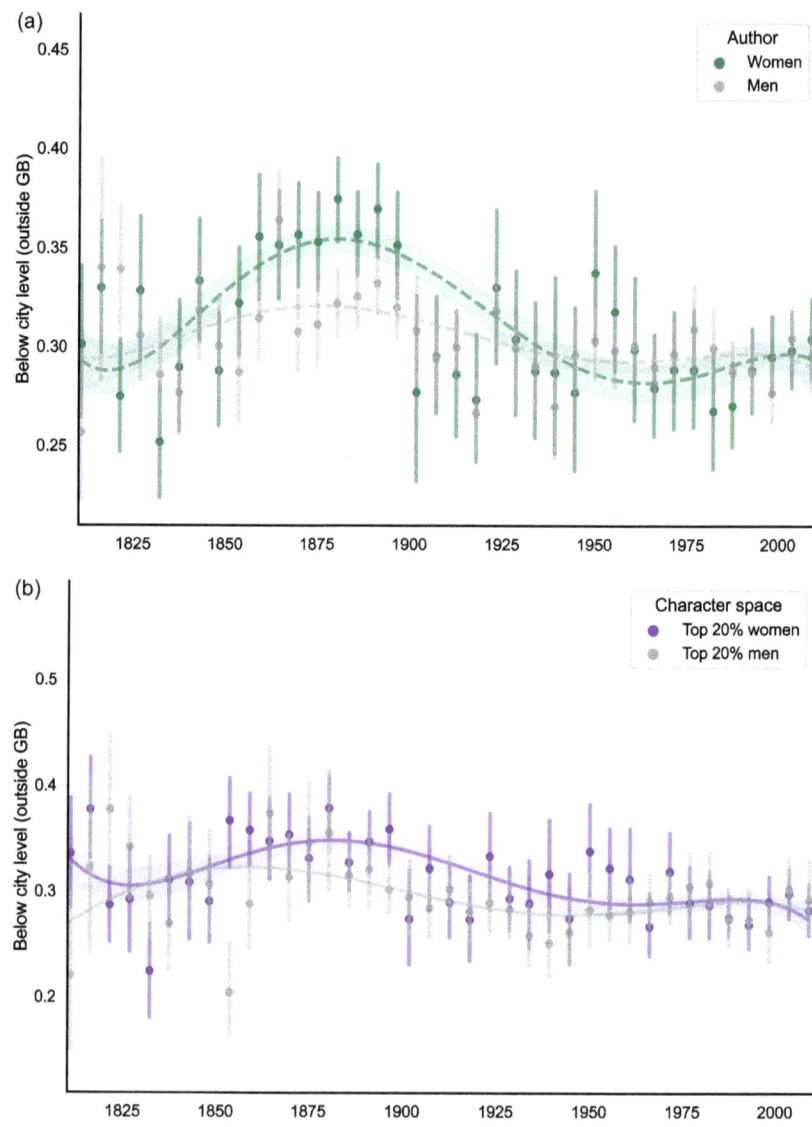

Figure 13 International subcity specificity by (a) author gender and (b) gendered character space.

(Figure 13(a)). A similar trend, albeit with delayed dates, is observable regarding gendered character space, where books that devoted most of their character space to women were more specific at the international subcity level than were those skewed toward men around 1870–1925 (Figure 13(b)). The rise in international subcity geographic specificity among women authors may be due to women's increasingly wide-ranging travel writing in the latter part of the nineteenth century. It makes for an interesting comparison with women writers' intensity of location mentions outside of the UK (Figure 7(a)); intensity dips in the same period (late nineteenth century) when specificity rises, then rises (at the beginning of the twentieth century) just when specificity dips. Taken together, these findings provide further indications that, in the twentieth century, women's writing about places beyond the UK became more political and less dominated than it had been by foreign locations as specific settings.

5.5 Conclusions

In sum, we find that fiction by and about women was generally more geographically specific than was fiction about men. Fiction by and about women was in fact more specific below the *country* level than that by and about men, both within and outside the UK. Specificity below the *city* level was more mixed. Throughout the nineteenth century and well into the twentieth, male authors were most specific below the city level within the UK and least specific below the city level internationally. These positions reversed in the latter half of the twentieth century, when the work of women writers became most specific below the city level within the UK and least specific internationally. *Character* space dominated by women, it should be noted, was more specific below the city level everywhere, though not always by a wide margin.

We also found that the commonplace narrative of increasing gender parity over time was again unsupported by our data. At the subnational level, both within and outside the UK, the difference between author- and character-space gender groups hardly varied over 200 years. At the subcity level, there was no consistent pattern. Instead, we find fluctuations determined by differing attention to international and domestic locations in apparent response to historical events ranging from wars and (de)colonization to political rivalry and human migration.

Finally, we return to the highest-level question we raised at the beginning of the section: is there a general trade-off in British fiction between a book's raw quantity of geographic attention (its intensity) and the detail or quality of that attention (its specificity)? Or do those aspects of geographic investment generally move together? The answer is two-fold, as shown in Figure 14. Internationally, the relationship is inverse: more geographic attention is accompanied by lower geographic specificity. Within the UK, the direction of the relationship depends on the level of intensity. When intensity is low, rising attention is accompanied by greater specificity. Beyond a certain point (around 150 to 300 location occurrences per 100,000 words), however, this relationship inverts so that it resembles the international case, with rising attention accompanied by falling specificity.

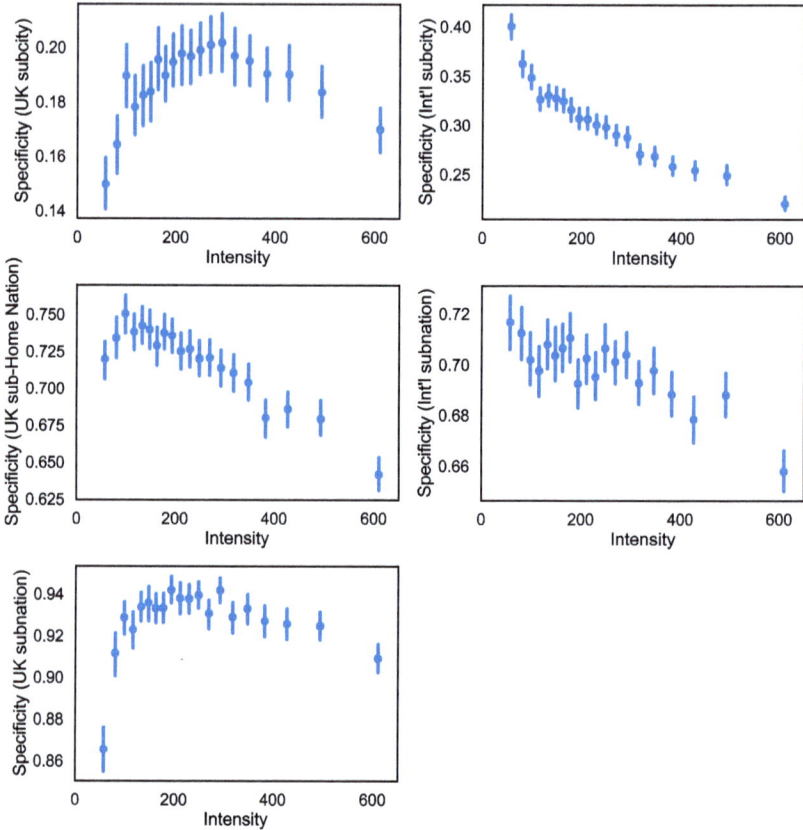

Figure 14 Five measures of geographic specificity as a function of intensity.

What should we make of these relationships? In the international case, we're likely seeing the combined influences of travel literature, itinerant plots, and political investments, each of which tends to produce a more geographically superficial treatment of a large number of locations outside Britain. This is in opposition to the detailed but comparatively brief set of locations required to locate stationary characters in geographic space. It isn't hard to imagine exceptions to these trends, but they hold consistently in aggregate when authors engage the world beyond Britain's borders.

In the British domestic case, we observe the same trend for geographically intensive books, which behave as if there exists a rough upper bound on the amount of setting-level detail that fits within the constraints of a novel. If a book talks about many places, it simply can't describe each of them in much detail. At the lower end of the intensity range, we find the opposite relationship, with books adding specificity as they devote more of their attention to geography.

When they address locations within the UK, British novels have generally treated geographic investment as a matter of increasing depth and detail, until they eventually reach a point (or a zone) past which geography becomes less a matter of specific settings than it is an apparent proxy for other concerns (mobility, displacement, politics, war, and so on).

6 The Gendering of Public and Private Spaces

Decades of feminist scholarship have examined how gender – and other aspects of cultural identity – shapes experience of and access to particular locations. Perhaps inevitably, those varied experiences shape in turn what kinds of stories are told by what kinds of people – stories that, in an endless feedback loop, influence lived spatial experience. An area of keen debate has concerned the degree to which women of nineteenth- and early twentieth-century Europe and America could make use of public space. Janet Wolff represented one pole in the debate when she argued that the "literature of modernity describes the experience of men. It is essentially a literature about transformations in the public world ... of work, politics and city life ... from which women were excluded, or in which they were practically invisible."[34] Others have been quick to point out the multiple ways in which women were participating in that public world despite the fact that, as Susan Buck-Morss put it, "all women who loitered [in public] risked being seen as whores" ("Flaneur" 111). In the wake of these debates, there remain pressing questions about women's access to public space and their degree of geographic mobility.

First among these issues is the doctrine of separate spheres, the well established view that, in the nineteenth century (among those classes who could afford it), men and women increasingly occupied distinct spheres: men the "public" world of work, government, and urban life and women the "private" world of the home and the suburb.[35] How rigid was that divide, as indicated by the comparative geographies of men and women writers and in books about men and about women? Can we observe in fiction the moment or period when women gained greater access to public space, and how closely that access approximated men's, if it ever did? If, by the early twentieth century, as critical consensus would suggest, women were increasingly present in public spaces and enjoyed increasing geographic mobility, then we might expect to see

---

[34] Wolff, "Invisible Flâneuse," 37. The target of Wolff's influential critique is the discourse of modernity as practiced by male historians, sociologists, and cultural critics who ignore the arenas in which women were present in their focus on public space.

[35] The doctrine of separate spheres began to gain strength as early as the middle of the eighteenth century, according to Martha Vicinus (*Independent Women*), and was at its height in the middle of the nineteenth century.

fictional representations of geographic gender differences weakening over time.[36]

Our findings about public and private spaces largely confirm the strength of separate-sphere ideology, even as its influence is complicated by the role of genre. However, they *counter* assumptions of progress in gender-spatial equity. We also find that separate-sphere ideology had a more complex spatial expression than is frequently assumed. We argue that semi-public spaces (for example, shops, restaurants, or vehicles of public transport), about which men and women authors differ in their alignment with gendered characters, are under-appreciated in gender-based approaches to urban space, which, influenced by the cultural importance of the *flâneur*, have often focused on wholly public streets (Gleber, *Art*; Elkin, *Flâneuse*). Scholars have turned increasingly to in-between places like restaurants, buses, and cabs; computational research offers new methods to explore their importance in the literary history of women's mobility.[37] In the last portion of this section we elucidate gender trends in literary geography through close analysis to the surprisingly high degree of attention paid to domestic space in several novels known for their engagements with urban life and to the under-appreciated role of vehicles of transportation in women's negotiation of public space and the home.

6.1 Measuring Attention to Public and Private Space

Measuring attention to "public" and "private" spaces requires first defining those terms with spatial rather than geographic referents. Most homes in literature, after all, aren't locatable to particular geographic coordinates. We sought to identify references to interior, domestic spaces regardless of whether they could be found on a map. We thus counted mentions of specific terms that we unite under the term "home spaces": *bedroom, kitchen, parlour, drawing-room, flat,* and *bedsit* (and their plurals and variant spellings). To assess representations of public space, we counted occurrences of outdoor places often used for travel, leisure, and gathering: *street, lane, road, avenue, square,* and *plaza*. We term these, collectively, "streets and squares."[38] To count mentions of our generic terms of interest, we used HathiTrust Research Center extracted

---

[36] Anna Snaith expresses the prevalent view when she writes, "not until the latter half of the nineteenth and the early twentieth centuries did women become a significant presence in the public realm" (*Virginia Woolf*, 16).

[37] Scholars have recently devoted particular attention to technologies of movement. See Grossman; Parkins; Vadillo; Thacker; Gavin and Humphries.

[38] The lists of terms supplied here are complete. Unless otherwise indicated, the same is true of other term lists provided in the text. Full lists of terms are also available in the online supplementary materials.

features files, which are page-level bags of words, each word tagged with its contextual part of speech.

As critical discourse led us to expect, we found that male authors and characters were more closely aligned with public roads and byways. Overall, male authors mentioned streets and squares about 27% more than did women authors (Figure 15(a)). Texts mostly about men referenced them a bit more yet than did those mostly about women (nearly 30% more; Figure 15(b)). On average over the centuries of our study, men and women writers agreed in this gendered gap (mentioning street spaces about 20% more in books about men than in those about women). However, in the 1901–50 period, when the status of women on the street was undergoing rapid change, the gap disappeared in the work of women writers. That is, while men continued to mention streets and related terms 21% more in their books about men than in those about women, women authors mentioned these spaces roughly equally in both kinds of books, perhaps indicating their sense that public spaces were now available to women and men alike.[39]

Use of street terms – and of nearly all the generic place terms that we discuss in this section – increased over time. While the rise of street terms may be partially attributed to urbanization, the increase in generic spatial terms is part of a broader phenomenon that has been observed by other researchers: "hard" or concrete terms increased throughout the nineteenth and twentieth centuries even as more abstract ideas decreased over the same period. Literature became more physical and less metaphysical over time.[40]

While the greater association of men with public spaces throughout the period is expected, it is surprising that we see so little convergence of the lines over time. Public space terms did become increasingly prominent in books about women throughout most of the period (with a possible small drop-off after 2000; Figure 15(b)), but they increased nearly in parallel with use in books about men. Only in the last decades of the twentieth century do we see any evidence that the two groups were drawing closer together, a trend that appears to reverse in the first decade of the twenty-first century. If public spaces were becoming increasingly available to

---

[39] After about 1950, however, male authors decreased the difference between masculine- and feminine-skewed texts with respect to street spaces, while women authors increasingly differentiated them. Women authors' erasure of gendered difference in public spaces in the 1901–50 period reverses the pattern we found in men and women writers' assessment of gender difference with respect to international locations. As discussed in Section 4, women authors consistently differentiated international attention between books about women and those about men more strongly than did male authors.

[40] The increasing concretization of literature was first observed at scale in Heuser and Le-Khak and further developed in Underwood and Sellers and in Underwood, *Distant Horizons*.

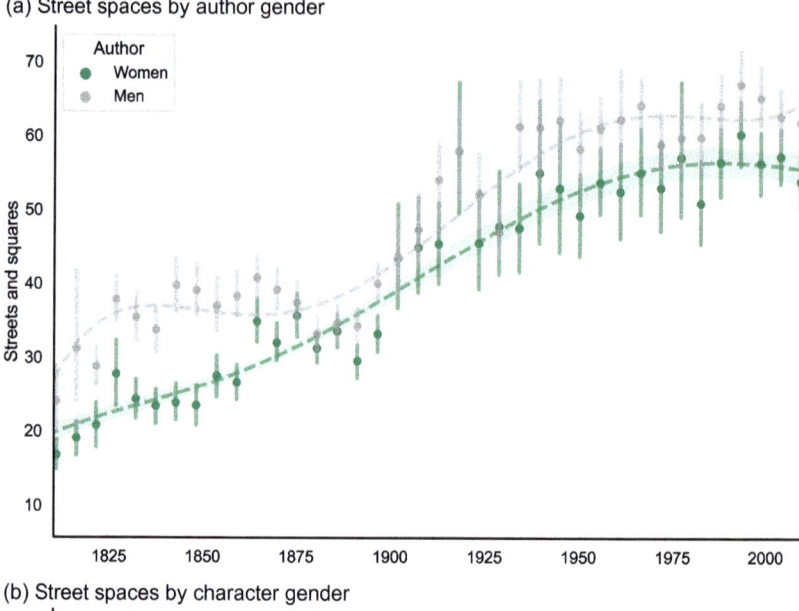

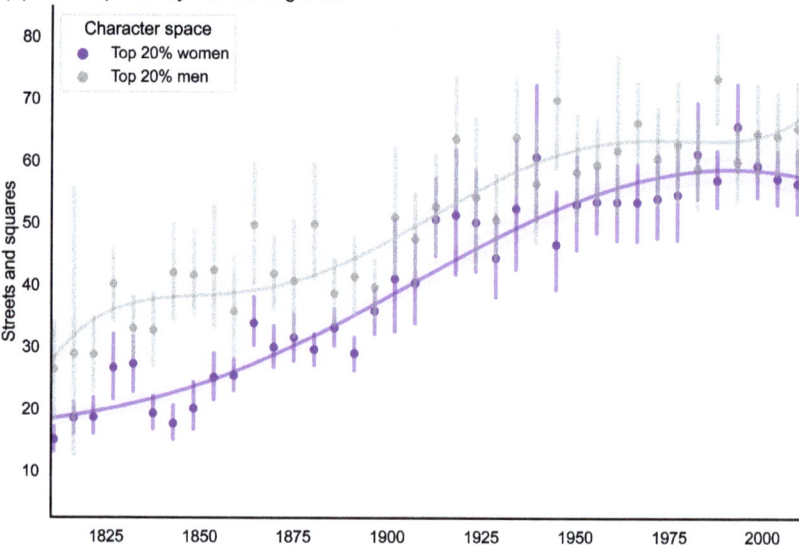

Figure 15 Gendered use of selected public and private spaces over time. In each subplot of this figure, the y axis indicates the average number of times that selected groups of words appear per 100,000 words in each five-year span. In (a) and (b), we plot the frequency of "street" words; in (c) and (d), the frequency of "home" words.

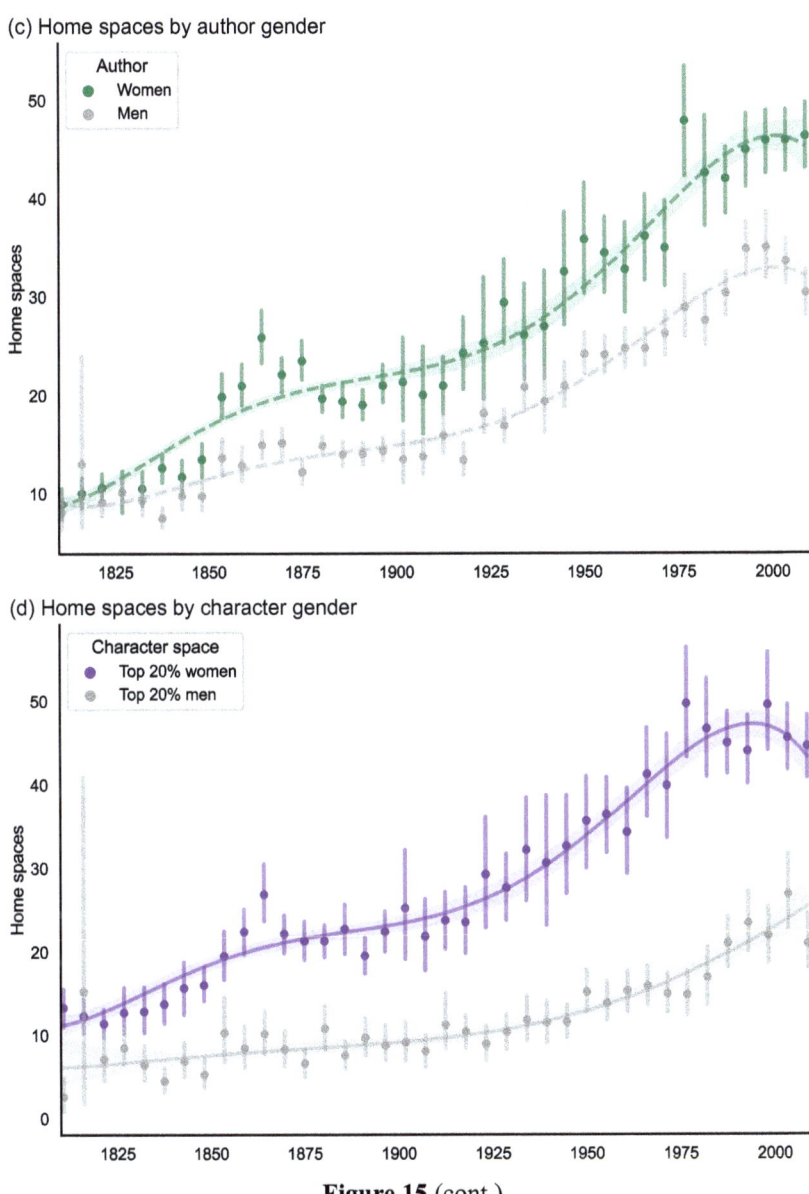

Figure 15 (cont.)

fictional women over time, they remained more associated with men than with women.

If men were as disproportionately connected with public street space as we suspected, so, too, were women more connected with private spaces. Women authors were much more likely to mention private domestic interiors, particularly after 1850 (Figure 15(c)). However, the gendering of private spaces was more a function of character gender than it was of authorial gender. The difference in attention to homes between books about women and those about men was more than 16 percentage points (compared to 6.5 percentage points in the case of authors; Figure 15(c–d)). Overall, fiction enriched in women characters mentioned locations within the home 123% more than did fiction enriched in men.

Men and women writers associated such spaces with women characters at similarly high rates.[41] In this case – and in most others – character gender rather than author gender emerges as the primary determinant of spatial attention. Home spaces could of course be public forums as well as private ones, as critics such as Lynn Walker have shown. But the divergence of gendered associations with domestic spaces in all books, and their increasing prominence in books that were mostly about women, in the nineteenth century suggests the force of the Victorian celebration of the home as women's retreat from the world.

6.2 Semi-Public Spaces

While the space of public streets and private homes divided cleanly by gender, semi-public spaces were another matter. We examined several types of semi-public spaces, locations that were ostensibly open to all, though often at a financial cost or with expectation of purchase. These included drinking places (*bar, tavern, pub*), eating places (*café, restaurant*), urban vehicles of public transportation (*omnibus, bus, tram*), cabs (*cab, taxi, taxicab, hansom*), trains (*railroad, railway, train*), shops (*shop, arcade*), parks (*park*), and religious spaces (*church, parsonage, temple*, and many more), as well as the plural forms of each of these terms. We found interesting patterns in these semi-public spaces, from strong, unambiguous gender associations in some cases to complex differences between gendered identities in others.

Unsurprisingly, for those familiar with British cultural history, drinking places were gendered male by both authors and characters (Figure 16). They were almost the only case we found in which authorial gender difference was greater than character-space gender difference, likely reflecting more limited access to those

---

[41] The absence of difference is of note, particularly in contrast to the case of streets and squares, where the two groups of writers disagreed profoundly regarding the strength of masculine associations with street spaces. Were women authors more aware of, and therefore more insistent about, the differences between men's and women's occupation of such public spaces than were male authors, even as they agreed with male authors in how much more home spaces were associated with women?

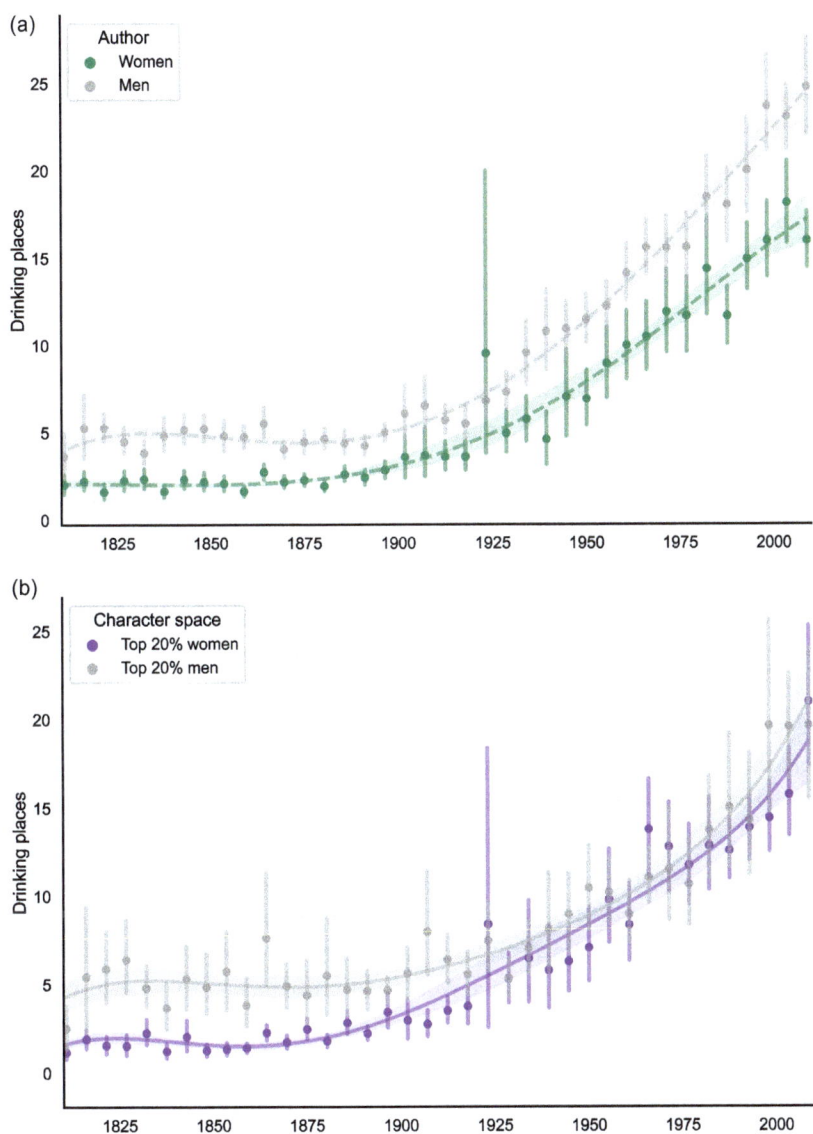

Figure 16 Drinking places by (a) author gender and (b) character gender.

locations for women authors, especially earlier in the period. The only other type of location in which men and women authors differed more than did books divided by differently gendered character space was the club, a conventional sphere in British culture for men's homosocial bonds.[42] While author gender remained a strong

---

[42] As Evans argues (*Threshold Modernism*, ch. 4), clubs for women were an important social force in late nineteenth century Britain, but they never achieved the cultural importance of the original old boys' clubs.

predictor of the use of drinking spaces, its predictive power lessened with the passage of time. What we might call the "drinking gap" between gender-skewed *texts*, on the other hand, closed by the mid-twentieth century. That is, books about women drew closer to those about men in their frequency of reference to drinking sites during the interwar decades and have remained close ever since.

There were several kinds of semi-public spaces that male authors mentioned more, but which they associated more often with women characters, including eating spaces and shopping spaces. While male authors were decisive in using spaces of consumption (whether to buy or to eat, though not to drink) at higher rates in their books about women, women authors did *not* show any statistically meaningful difference between gendered character space in this regard. Men also wrote more about spaces of transportation, particularly about specific London stations and, except in the case of trains (where there is no statistically significant difference), they associated spaces of transportation more with books about women than about men.[43] Women authors, on the other hand, only showed a significant gendered association with character space in the case of cabs, which they, like male authors, aligned more with women characters. Vehicles of public transit and popular London stations were not only associated more with women characters in the period overall but they became increasingly concentrated in books about women throughout the twentieth century (Figure 17). Cabs came more quickly – as early as the 1860s – to show an association with books about women, which increased until the late twentieth century, when books about men began to catch up (Figure 18).

Cabs are not only of interest for the analysis of gender and semi-public space generally but, because they have already received penetrating historical and literary analysis, they are a fruitful subject for methodological comparison and synergy.[44] Focusing on Virginia Woolf and other modernist women writers, Anne Fernald argues that cabs allowed modern women "maximum power as spectators when it was still brave for a woman to be a pedestrian" (214). Without interference from the male gaze, women could "simultaneously observe the world and imagine [their] place in it" (215). Our analysis of many thousands of books over two centuries demonstrates a longer history for a phenomenon Fernald identifies in the modernist era.[45] And while our study

---

[43] We grouped these generic spaces of transportation into three categories: vehicles of urban public transportation, cabs, and trains. As an alternate measure, we also counted references to a handful of well-known London train and Underground stations (Waterloo Station, Victoria Station, Paddington Station, Euston Station, and St. Pancras Station).

[44] We focus on Fernald. Other work on cabs in literary history includes Stokes and sources on urban transportation cited previously.

[45] Of course, the reasons behind the numbers may have shifted. As privately owned automobiles became more pervasive in the twentieth century, taking cabs may have become increasingly

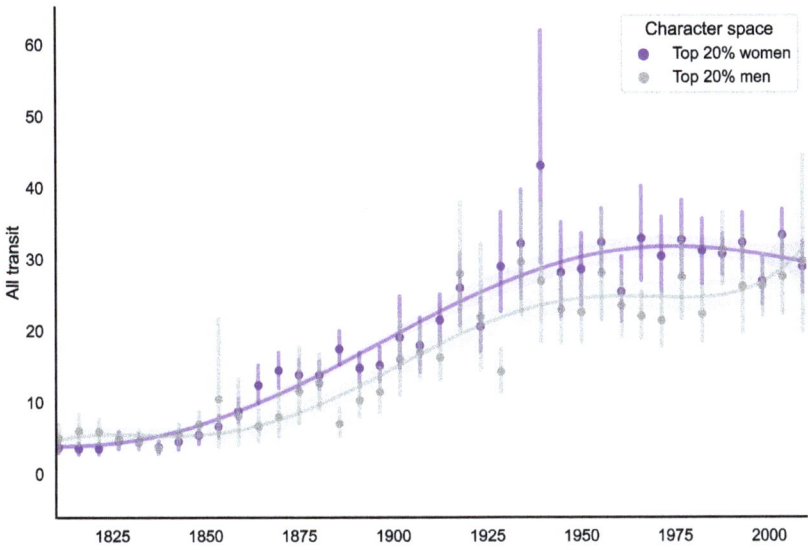

Figure 17 Urban public transport by gendered character space.

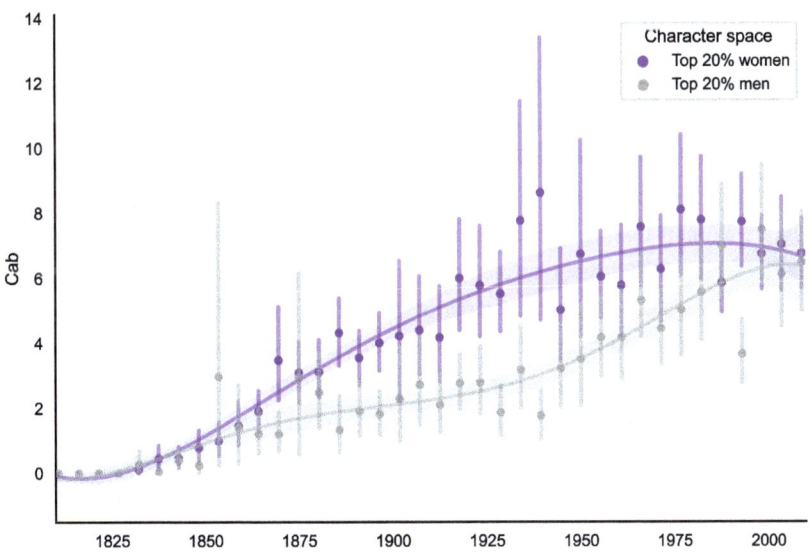

Figure 18 Cabs by gendered character space.

confirms at broad scale what Fernald has noticed in well-known texts – that cabs are associated with women characters – we find a more complex relationship with authorial gender than Fernald's article implies through its focus on texts by

---

a sign of having fewer financial resources than those who could get around in their own car. A more pedestrian explanation may be footwear, as women's heels became higher and less suitable for walking.

women writers. Male authors not only mentioned cabs somewhat more than did women authors across the period of our study, but they associated cabs with women characters at a higher rate than did women authors. We hypothesize that the same forces that led male authors to associate streets and other public by-ways with men may have prompted their association of cabs with women, including a heightened sense of the dangers suggested by women in wholly public space and perhaps a sense that women did not belong there. That is, male authors may have associated women characters more with cabs because they didn't see women as walkers.

But these findings about what we've termed "semi-public" spaces raise questions about what we mean when we talk about public, as compared to private, space. For one can consider restaurants, shops, and buses as participating as fully in the experience of public life as streets. Indeed, such locations are perhaps more likely than streets to give rise to interactions among strangers. The same may be said of parks, which, as a generic term, *and* as specifically named London parks, were – intriguingly – most associated with women. This alignment between parks and books about women calls to mind historical cultural associations of women with nature, even as parks were also urban social spaces of widely varying accessibility and privacy.[46] There was little difference in the degree to which men and women authors mentioned parks, both in generic terms and in reference to our set of named London parks.[47] But there was a dramatic difference in how both men and women authors associated them with gendered character space. References to generic parks were 58% higher in texts about women than in those about men, while references to specific London parks were 103% higher across the same split. In the case of women-authored texts alone, references to named parks were 236% higher in books about women than in those about men; that is, women authors associated parks with women-centered character space *more than three times* more than they did with male-centered character space. Male authors tempered this difference, mentioning parks in books about women roughly twice as much as they did in books about men, largely because they increased the allotment of parks in books about men. Parks thus provide an interesting counterpoint to the gendering of spaces of consumption (businesses for eating and shopping), which male authors

---

[46] For more on parks as social spaces that held in tension qualities of public space and private space, see Evans, "Alternative Geographies and Urban Parks: Duse Mohamed Ali and Yoshio Markino in Imperial London" and Evans, "The Promises and Limits of Virginia Woolf's London Parks."

[47] In the period overall, generic parks were mentioned slightly more by women authors than by male authors; our set of named London parks were mentioned at similar rates by men and women authors. The named London parks include well-known green spaces, mostly in central London: Hyde Park, Kew Gardens, Kensington Gardens, Green Park, St. James' Park, and Regent's Park, along with variant spellings.

associated more with women characters than did women authors. Further, if streets were not as available to women as they were to men, it seems that parks were helping to make up the deficit, providing one explanation – in the form of urban green space – for how, as we will explore in Section 7, the city could function as a territory that was unexpectedly open to women.[48]

We've seen that widespread associations of masculinity with public space – defined as streets and other byways – and femininity with private space – understood as domestic interiors – are confirmed by the results. Parks, however, provide one instance in which our expectations are reversed, calling for a reevaluation of the gendered discourse of "public" and "private" space. If public streets and private interiors conform to gender expectations overall, there are yet interesting variations between men and women authors' representations of their relative alignment with each character gender group. Semi-public spaces, too, emerge as areas for future research. Overall, women authors seem to have put their men and women characters in most semi-public urban spaces at roughly equal rates, while male authors populated these spaces more with women characters.

"Religious spaces" are an interesting exception to this trend in semi-public spaces. Women authors – who mentioned such words as "church," "parsonage," and "temple" (among others) about 10% more than did male authors – used them more in books about men than in those about women. Male authors showed no such difference, using them roughly equally in books of both categories. A closer look reveals that the difference in men and women authors' character gender associations with religious spaces is a product of the twentieth century. In the nineteenth century, when religious spaces were a part of most people's daily experience, there was no significant difference in use by gender. In the twentieth century, when "church" became less important as an everyday space, it may have become more remarkable as a highly gendered institution, at least in the eyes of women authors. Religious spaces are also exceptional in their lack of referential growth over time. Whereas every other type of generic space we measured occurred more frequently as the twentieth century progressed, the rate of references to religious spaces was flat or declining (Figure 19).

We've also seen that levels of gender-geographic difference regarding public and private spaces have remained surprisingly consistent over time. It is not

---

[48] In Evans and Wilkens, we report that foreign-born writers of color were much more likely to name London's major parks than were both native-born writers and foreign-born white writers. This commonality between foreign-born writers of color and women in British fiction suggests that parks may have been more welcoming or allowed more freedom for those less advantaged by cultural hierarchies than other public and semi-public locations. Evans develops this argument in "Alternative Geographies" and "Promises."

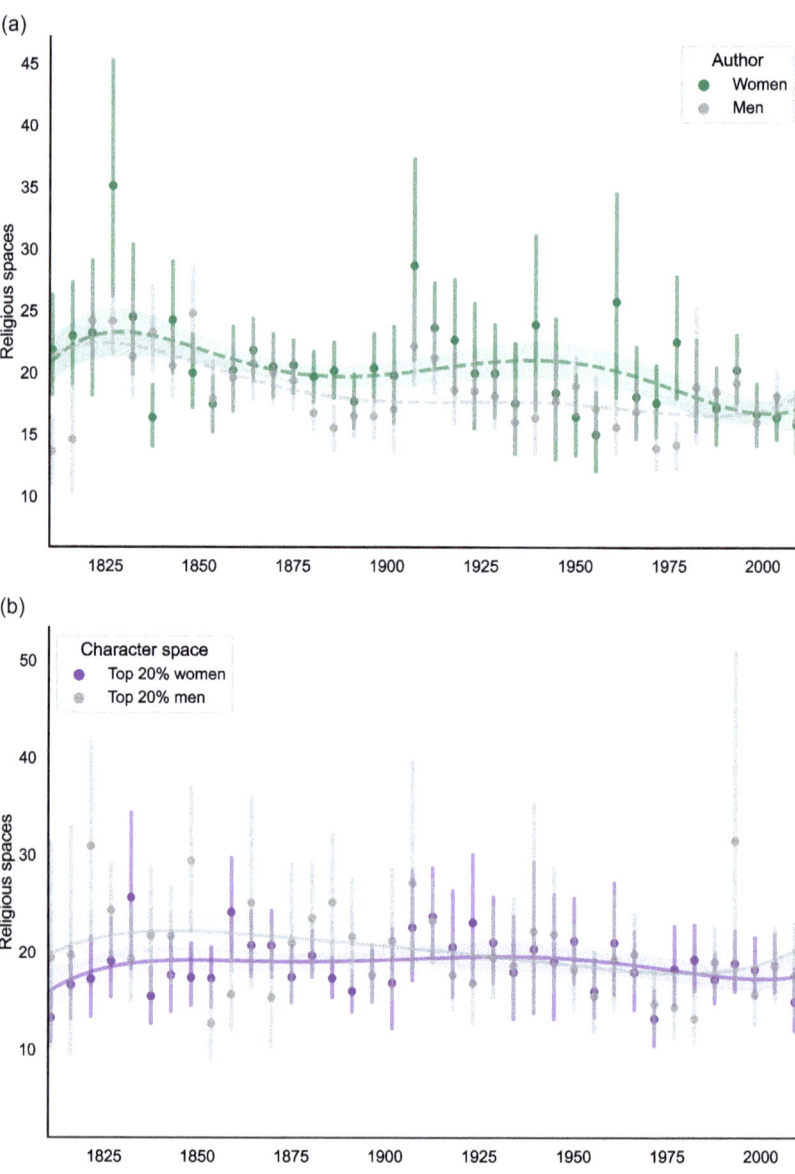

Figure 19 Religious spaces by (a) author gender and (b) gendered character space.

often the case that men and women, whether authors or characters, drew closer together in their spatial associations. If mentions of locations are a proxy for where people feel comfortable, we have not seen the degree of progress we expected. Indeed, the gender gap in characters' association with private domestic spaces has remained constant or even widened, depending on how we measure it, rather than narrowed, over the roughly two hundred years in this study, a finding that calls for further exploration concerning the valences of home spaces, especially in the contemporary period.

The case of homes also provides an example of how differences between genders were often more pronounced in the fictional world. What is a slight difference between men and women authors may be a pronounced difference between texts that emphasize those genders. Regarding mentions of public spaces, for instance, in the case of authorial gender, men and women appear to draw close together in the fraction of their mentions of public space between about 1875 and 1935, but their gendered characters don't share much of this narrowing of the gap. As we discussed in regard to international attention (Section 4), there appear to be gender-typed roles that authors use for their characters, but by which authors themselves are less constrained.

6.3 Public and Private Spaces in Practice

How might the detection of large-scale patterns in the space of British fiction – in this section, the degree of attention to public and private spaces in different eras and by differently gendered groups of authors and characters – increase our understanding of an individual text, the standard unit of analysis in literary study? The remainder of this section explores this question through Joseph Conrad's well-known novel *The Secret Agent* (1907), which appeared in the middle of our period. Though Conrad described the book, in its dedication to H. G. Wells, as a "simple tale of the nineteenth century," it has been celebrated as a proto-modernist work in which the machinery of plot takes second place to psychological exposition. Like its even better known modernist counterparts, such as James Joyce's *Ulysses* and Woolf's *Mrs. Dalloway*, Conrad's novel explores and diagnoses the modern psyche alongside the modern city.

Indeed, *The Secret Agent* is often celebrated, with good cause, as one of the great city novels. Set entirely in London, it feels like a novel of the city, its clandestine plots, and its exterior spaces. Many of its most memorable scenes (the accidental encounter of Inspector Heat and the Professor; Winnie pleading with Ossipon to help her escape after she kills her husband) occur on public streets. Verloc's commitment to protecting the city's "opulence and luxury" is established early in the novel through his walk alongside Hyde Park to Knightsbridge and the embassy in Chesham Square (51), Winnie's protective aspirations for her brother are summarized by her pleasure in seeing him walk with her husband down the street, imagining that, in appearance, they "[m]ight be father and son" (179), and the novel ends with Ossipon walking blindly through the streets, while the Professor "walked, too .... He passed on unsuspected and deadly, like a pest in the street full of men" (269). The novel's pivotal event is an explosion in Greenwich Park, a mishap of what was intended to seize the public's attention.

Yet, despite the novel's emphasis on the city's public spaces, computational analysis reveals its remarkable degree of attention to domestic space. *The Secret Agent* ranks in the top 2% of books by frequency of home-space references. Notably, the novel is typical of its time in terms of its gendered character space; it allocates 28.7% of its gendered character space to women, near the period average of 29.5%. The surprising degree of private space in *The Secret Agent* brings our attention to Conrad's treatment of the "public" and the "private" and, thence, to how the novel undermines expected divisions between the two as conceptual as well as spatial terms. Private affairs turn out to have international repercussions and vice versa. Verloc's responsibility for the attempted bombing of the Greenwich Observatory is literally brought home when the police discover Verloc's address, written by Winnie with her "protecting passion," on a scrap of clothing salvaged among Stevie's remains (185). Stevie's death, through premature detonation of the bomb he carried, is the ultimate result of the pressure Verloc received from his foreign employers to earn his living as an *agent provocateur*. Verloc maintains that he never would have orchestrated the act of terrorism if he hadn't "felt certain that his wife would not even hear of going abroad." Though entwined with a tale of international intrigue, as the Assistant Commissioner observes, "From a certain point of view we are here in the presence of a domestic drama" (204).[49]

A closer look at the domestic spaces imagined in the novel reveals Conrad's emphasis on the thin, permeable boundary between public and private. It is appropriate that the Verlocs met in the rooming house kept by Winnie's mother, for their married home will also cross the border into business. The Verlocs' shop, with its illicit offerings, stands between the street and the house, as Conrad reminds us on several occasions (46–47, 188). Verloc's association with the city's anarchists, which really pays the bills, is fostered by meetings within the house, the men gathered around the fireplace, "the horse-hair armchair in which Mrs. Verloc's mother was generally privileged to sit" occupied by a self-defined "terrorist" with "toothless gums" (73–74). This overlapping of spatial purpose is dangerous for the house's occupants as things are overheard that shouldn't be: Stevie hears and is agitated by the anarchists talking; Winnie hears Verloc confess to Chief Inspector Heat his attempt to bomb the observatory and

---

[49] In fact, the novel's degree of international attention is relatively low; 44.5% of its named locations are outside the UK, whereas the average book in our corpus is 69.8% international. The paucity of international place names contributes to the novel's sense of claustrophobia. It is no wonder that Verloc's proposal to go abroad is a nonstarter for Winnie.

Heat's description of Stevie, "[b]lown to bits" (196). Most damningly for the supposed sanctity of the home, the Verlocs' very marriage is revealed to be, at least on one side, an economic transaction rather than a romantic union, Winnie having relinquished the man she loved to marry one who had the means and will to take in her brother Stevie and her mother. She was "capable of a bargain the mere suspicion of which would have been infinitely shocking to Mr. Verloc's idea of love" (232). Though Verloc is said to be "thoroughly domesticated," without "needs ... to take him much abroad" (47), his demeanor and behavior – his appearance in the shop with the "air of having wallowed, fully dressed, all day on an unmade bed" (46), his habit of wearing his overcoat at home – blur the boundary between public and private life. Though "it was in all essentials of domestic propriety and domestic comfort a respectable home," the novel continually shows us its failings (185). Suitably, then, Winnie stabs her husband with a kitchen knife as he "reposed characteristically, clad in his outdoor garments" (232).

If private and public mingle within the Verlocs' home, outdoor spaces carry an uncanny echo of domestic space. This is most clear in the encounter between Chief Inspector Heat, who has just examined the wreckage of Stevie's body, and the Professor, who supplied the explosives that blew him up. The men meet by chance in a dark, narrow alley in which "yawned the cavern of a second-hand-furniture dealer, where, deep in the gloom of a sort of narrow avenue winding through a bizarre forest of wardrobes, with an undergrowth tangle of table legs, a tall pier-glass glimmered like a pool of water in a wood. An unhappy, homeless couch, accompanied by two unrelated chairs, stood in the open" (103). In the middle of the city, with the sounds of busier streets on each side, we are given a cluster of used furniture that conjures a forest that is also a home. When the men come face to face, it is "like a meeting in a side corridor of a mansion full of life" (104). While the encounter threatens the lives of both men, its setting echoes the novel's two other places of death. Its resemblance to a forest conjures Greenwich Park, where Stevie was blown up, most likely having stumbled over a tree root. (With horror, Winnie will imagine fragments of his body mixed with "smashed branches, torn leaves" [232–33].) The "unhappy, homeless" and "unrelated" second-hand furniture suggests the hollowness of the Verlocs' married home, founded upon a bargain now voided by Verloc's culpability for Stevie's death. Chronologically between the two violent killings, but narrated before both of them, the scene encapsulates the obscure danger that menaces both the city and the home.

Conrad's is not the only novel known for its engagement with the city to have a surprisingly large portion of textual attention devoted to domestic space. Virginia Woolf's *Mrs. Dalloway* (1925) and Jean Rhys's *Voyage in the Dark*

(1934) also meet this description, falling comfortably in the top 10% of books ranked by frequency of home-space references. There has been but modest attention paid to the home spaces of these novels, especially when set against the plentiful scholarly assessments of their urban environments – a fact that comes into view when we become aware of how outsized is their interest in domestic interiors compared to other novels. By surfacing aspects of well-known texts that have received little attention, we showcase one of the most tangible benefits of computational research. To the work of those scholars who have noted the role of homes in these texts, we add in closing a brief consideration of how other statistically outstanding kinds of places – notably, cabs and vehicles of public transit – function in relation to domestic spaces.[50]

Voyage in the Dark and *Mrs. Dalloway* are not only strikingly attentive to domestic interiors, but are also exceptionally attuned to vehicles of transportation. *Voyage in the Dark*, Jean Rhys's powerful short novel of a young woman adrift in the modern city, ranks in the top 0.3% of all books in our study by its frequency of mentions of cabs. *Mrs. Dalloway* falls in the top 20% in regard to cabs and in the top 10% in regard to urban vehicles of public transit. With the notable exception of the cab in *Mrs. Dalloway*, whose occupant remains an unknown emblem of state power, these vehicles are significant spaces for women characters in both novels. They are liminal spaces, on the threshold of – and the route between – the home and other, more public, spaces. Though "no Dalloways came down the Strand daily," when Elizabeth Dalloway ventures there by omnibus, she finds she wants to have a profession (137). At the other end of the social spectrum, Anna Morgan's frequent travel by taxi in *Voyage in the Dark* is generally connected with the men she sees. When alone or with friends Maudie, Ethel, or Laurie, Anna most often travels by Tube, bus, or foot. In her first sexual relationship, with Walter Jeffries, they go together in taxis to restaurants and shows and their evenings end in the early morning with her cab ride from his home to hers. After that relationship ends, Anna's first-person narration nearly always reports the taking of a taxi when she goes out with or meets a man, the repetition of the action echoing the futility of her cycling through increasingly precarious relationships and one unwelcoming, even dangerous, living space after another. Taking a taxi to meet Jeffries when he's breaking up with her, she notices "the houses on either side of the street were small and dark and then they were big and dark but all exactly alike" (96). The sentiment recurs (e.g., "all the houses outside in the street were the same – all alike" (103)), "the houses all exactly alike" (179) becoming a motif for

---

[50] For work on Jean Rhys and domestic interiors see GoGwilt; Mullholland. Scholars who have considered domestic spaces in Woolf's oeuvre broadly include Peach; Snaith, *Virginia Woolf*; and Zink.

Anna's lack of choice, her entrapment in an endless cycle of rooms and cabs, that leave her either dying from a botched abortion or, in the words of a visiting doctor, about to start "all over again" (188).[51]

As we noted in Section 6.2, cabs and vehicles of public transit, like home spaces, were most associated with women's character space. But of course, their meaning is not stable. Whereas *Mrs. Dalloway* celebrates how the omnibus can be a vehicle for exploration and self-realization for a young woman temporarily escaping from the safety and constraints of the family home, *A Voyage in the Dark* imagines cabs as passageways between home spaces and public spaces that reinforce how little protection Anna's homes provide her. Like Winnie's house in *The Secret Agent*, Anna's homes are functional rather than ideal, providing shelter without safety. The surprisingly high degree of attention to homes in all of these city novels is an indication of the interconnections they reveal between public urban space and the supposedly private domestic interior, interconnections that appear to vary additionally along axes of social and marital status. Vehicles of transport may be the conduit between the spaces, for good or for ill: a significant transition zone or a binding link.

***

We began this section noting the urgent questions around women's access to and relationship with public space, given their historical associations with private space and of men with public ones – questions that are no less important now than in the nineteenth and twentieth centuries. We wondered how rigid was the spatial divide between men and women, as indicated by their fiction. While some of the broad outlines of separate sphere ideology were confirmed by computational analysis of many thousands of fictional volumes, the process directed our attention to outliers (for example, books that were unusually rich in domestic spaces) that undermine traditional distinctions between public spaces for men and private spaces for women. Semi-public spaces also emerged as productive areas for continued research. In this section we began to explore the complex gender dynamics of cabs and vehicles of public transportation in British fiction that unsettle public/private, masculine/feminine demarcations. Quantitative analysis that revealed books with unusually high rates of reference to both homes and vehicles of transport provided new insights about how, for women, such vehicles not only brokered divisions between home and the world, but also broke them down.

---

[51] GoGwilt makes a similar point about the commonalities between the street, the interior, and character interiority in an essay discussing Conrad's *The Shadow-Line: A Confession* and Rhys's *Good Morning Midnight*.

7 Gender and the City

If the doctrine of separate spheres continues to inform expectations of where men and women are found, a closely related concept holds that cities are predominantly masculine environments. After all, what has more streets and other public byways – generic spatial terms that, as we saw in the last section, have been consistently associated with men – than cities? In fact, as we noted in the introduction, the association of urban space with masculinity is longstanding, as, indeed, is the association of natural space with femininity. New methods and an expanded corpus reveal a different story.

In this section we examine what expanding the scope of analysis may do for our understanding of the relationship between gender and urban space. What light might it shed on the widespread consensus that the late nineteenth and early twentieth centuries in Britain witnessed the increased presence of women in urban space and that the city was then (and remains today) a profoundly different environment for men and women?[52] Can we better understand the gender associations of urban space and its dialectical counterpart, natural space? How, if at all, have those associations changed through the centuries? We extend the previous section's comparative treatment of public space to focus on the city, combining generic public locations discussed there with geographic references measured using the methods detailed in Sections 3 and 4.

As in previous sections, we formulate questions with measurable outcomes:

1. To what extent did authorial gender predict the choice (or not) of an urban setting?
2. Did gender-skewed books differ in their tendency to use urban settings? That is, were books that were mostly about men or mostly about women more likely than the other group to reference cities?
3. Was the modernist era, with its strong urban associations, spatially distinct in any way from what came before or after it? Can we detect a historical shift in (extraliterary) spatial access reflected in where authors set their books and whom they chose to populate their cities?

The critical histories explored here and in the previous section expect authorial gender to play a significant role in urban representation. They also expect writing of the modernist era to demonstrate a greater engagement with urban

---

[52] See Parkins; Walker; Parsons; and Evans, *Threshold Modernism* for a focus on the transformative years between, roughly, the 1880s and the 1940s. For comparison with the contemporary city, see Elkin, who writes, "From Teheran to New York, from Melbourne to Mumbai, a woman still can't walk in the city the way a man can" (286).

space. Our findings undercut both of these stories even as they contradict many longstanding associations of men with urban space. Our results reveal the extent to which cities were the focal points for tales of women's encounters with an unpredictable modern world. When men wrote, it seems that the promises and perils of the urban environment were best explored through women's experiences. Urban settings often held different meanings for women writers as they wrote against the pervasive narrative of women's sexual danger in the city.

7.1 Calculating an Urban Metric

Our objective was to detect and count books that human readers would assess as "urban" in order to determine (1) the extent to which authorial gender predicted the choice (or not) of an urban setting and (2) how much that choice was correlated with books that used predominantly masculine or feminine character space. As we have throughout this study, we also sought to understand how patterns shifted over time, from 1800 to 2009.

The "urban metric" we designed balances two methods of measurement: a geographic method and a spatial one. The geographic method considers what fraction of all references to locations are – or are contained within – one of the world's most populous cities. The spatial method counts the number of references to generic locations associated with cities. We'll have more to say about both methods, but it's worth first considering the reasons for and implications of this dual focus. Geographic references provide important information about the story world and the narrative. Every experienced reader would expect a story set in central London to unfold differently, and with a different cast of characters, than one set in the Cotswolds. We reasoned, however, that the extent to which a book is experienced as one immersed in the urban environment or city living is not only a result of geographical references, but also of references to the features of any modern city: streets and traffic, crowds and places of entertainment. We chose to appraise the significance of both components equally, giving the same weight to a book's geographical setting and to its generic urban references. A different allocation of significance would have changed our findings, as we'll see when we break down these component parts.

We assembled our list of the world's most populous cities on a sliding scale, requiring larger populations for those cities further from Britain, the home territory of most of our writers under analysis. Within Britain, we included the eight cities that were the largest on average across the period 1800–2009: London, Birmingham, Glasgow, Liverpool, Bristol, Manchester, Sheffield, and Leeds. All had a population over 500,000 in 2023. We required a higher present-day population for European and American cities (750,000 and 3 million, respectively) and a higher one yet for cities elsewhere in the world (over 12 million for China and over 5 million for others). While including those cities British fiction was most likely to reference, the sliding scale kept the total number of cities to 100, a manageable number for hand review and a reasonable limit on places that *feel* both large and well known to many UK readers. We used the geolocation methods described in Section 3 to count the fraction of named locations that were one of the cities themselves or that were located within one of them.

Our generic urban locations might be located anywhere, though some – like "bedsit" – are more idiomatic in Britain. These terms included some of the words we have seen in previous sections and some we have not: *street, lane, square, road, avenue, plaza, omnibus, bus, tram, cab, taxi, taxicab, hansom, park, shop, arcade, crowd, office, museum, flat, bedsit, hotel, theatre, cinema, cabaret, symphony, orchestra, opera*, and *city* (as well as their plurals and variant spellings). While one can imagine cases in which any of these places could be located in a small town or rural environment, there is good reason to associate each of them more with urban than with nonurban environments.[53] One instance of any of the terms counted the same as any other. We might have chosen to weigh certain types of urban terms differently. For instance, since we know from work discussed in the previous section that terms associated with public byways (streets and so forth, which together account for about 40% of the total occurrences of our urban terms) are favored more by male authors and characters than by their women counterparts, we might have tempered that influence by decreasing the weight we gave to public streets. In our assessment, however, there was no reason to think that some of these words were any more likely to conjure urban space than any of the others.

A few better-known examples of books at the top end of the urban metric scale gives a sense of the range of settings even among books selected for their urban environments: Sherwood Anderson's *Windy McPherson's Son* (1916), in which the hero leaves Caxton, Iowa for Chicago; Ben Okri's *Stars of the New Curfew* (1989), a collection of stories set in Lagos and in various Nigerian villages; and Sue Gee's *Letters from Prague* (1994), which follows a woman and her daughter through Brussels, Berlin, and Prague.

---

[53] The list provided in the text is complete, though there are certainly other terms we might have included as well. The point, however, is not so much to be comprehensive as to identify a representative collection; large-scale comparisons across time and across groups of writers make the study robust to the effects of any particular term. As noted in section 6, the lists of terms supplied in the text are exhaustive unless otherwise indicated.

7.2 The Surprising Reversal of Urban and Natural Gender Associations

Our results were surprising. Despite the longstanding association of men with urban space, we found that books by men and by women referenced city spaces at close to equal rates throughout the two hundred plus years under study (Figure 20(a)). The first half of the twentieth century did show male authors using urban locations slightly more than did women, but the difference was slender and of marginal significance. More striking yet is the distinct preference for urban space among books mostly about women when compared to books mostly about men (Figure 20(b)). In fact, the same period (1901–1950) that saw a slight dip for women authors saw meaningfully more urban attention in women-centered character space. The reader will recall that this difference between author gender and gendered character space was repeated in other metrics we examined as well, such as uses of public and private space and of international and UK locations.

But the most surprising finding about gender and the metropole may be that it was *men's* authorial choices that accounted for the greater association between women characters and the city. Women authors showed no meaningful difference between books across predominantly gendered character space in their use of urban space, whereas male authors strongly correlated women-centered character space with cities. This calls for future research, but one explanation is suggested by the anxiety about women in the city that feminist scholars have noticed in texts by men. A selective sampling of books by men with character space skewed toward women that scored highly in the urban metric includes many tales about women subjugated or corrupted by economic hardship and sexual exploitation in the city, such as Walter M. Gallichan's *Like Stars That Fall* (1895) and Thomas Burke's *The Flower of Life* (1919) (in the top 10% and top 5%, respectively). H.G. Wells's *Ann Veronica* (1909) is a more familiar example of a male-authored book fascinated by the individual liberty and sexual danger for women in the metropole. In contrast, the smaller number of books by women that were high on the urban metric – including Ella Hepworth Dixon's *The Story of a Modern Woman* (1894), Dorothy Richardson's *The Tunnel* (1919), and Virginia Woolf's *The Years* (1937) (all in the top 15%) – often focused more on liberty for self development than on danger for women in the urban environment.[54] Some books had other concerns altogether, like Ellen Wilkinson's *Clash* (1929), a novel about labor organizing and one woman's choice of her work over a romantic partner who would require its abandonment.

---

[54] Women protagonists in these relatively well-known example texts face financial, but rarely sexual, precarity along with their freedom.

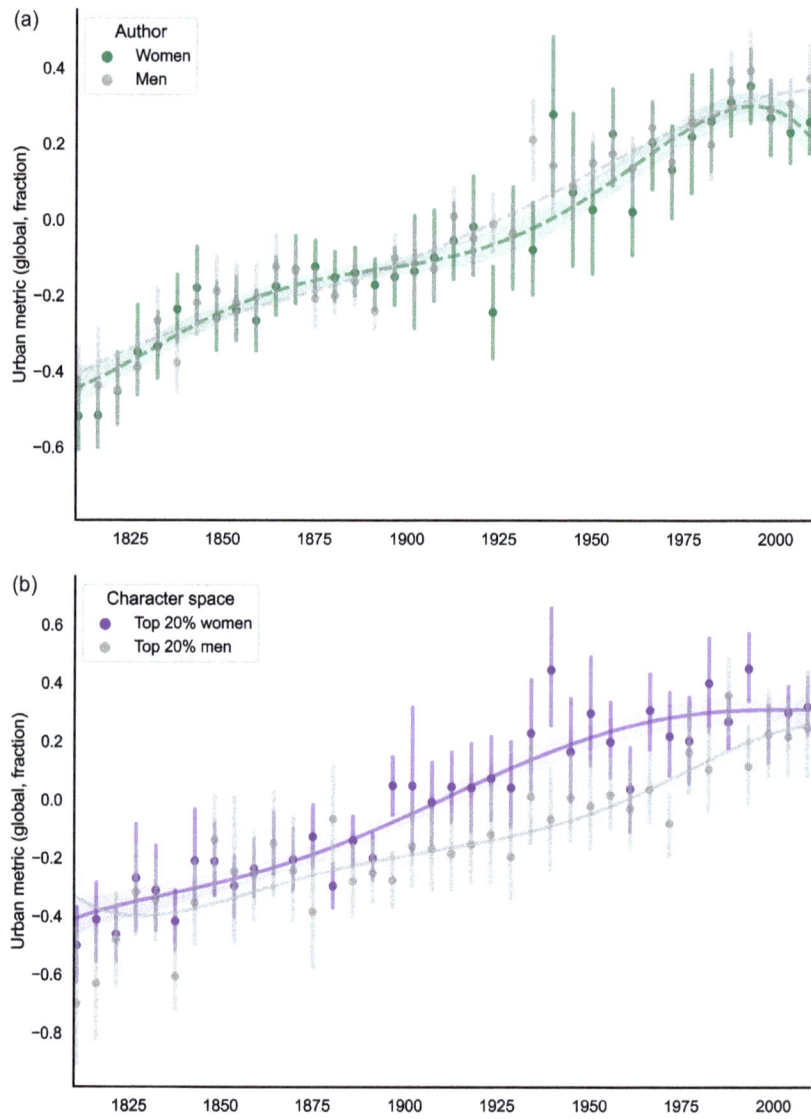

Figure 20 Global urban metric over time (a) by author gender and (b) by gendered character space. The metric is plotted as a z-score over all volumes in the corpus.

We'll return to women's treatment of cities and sexual danger in more detail at the end of this section.

The discovery that cities are aligned more with books about women than with those about men finds an equally surprising corollary when it comes to natural locations. When we counted references to generic sites such as *mountain, forest,*

Gender and Literary Geography

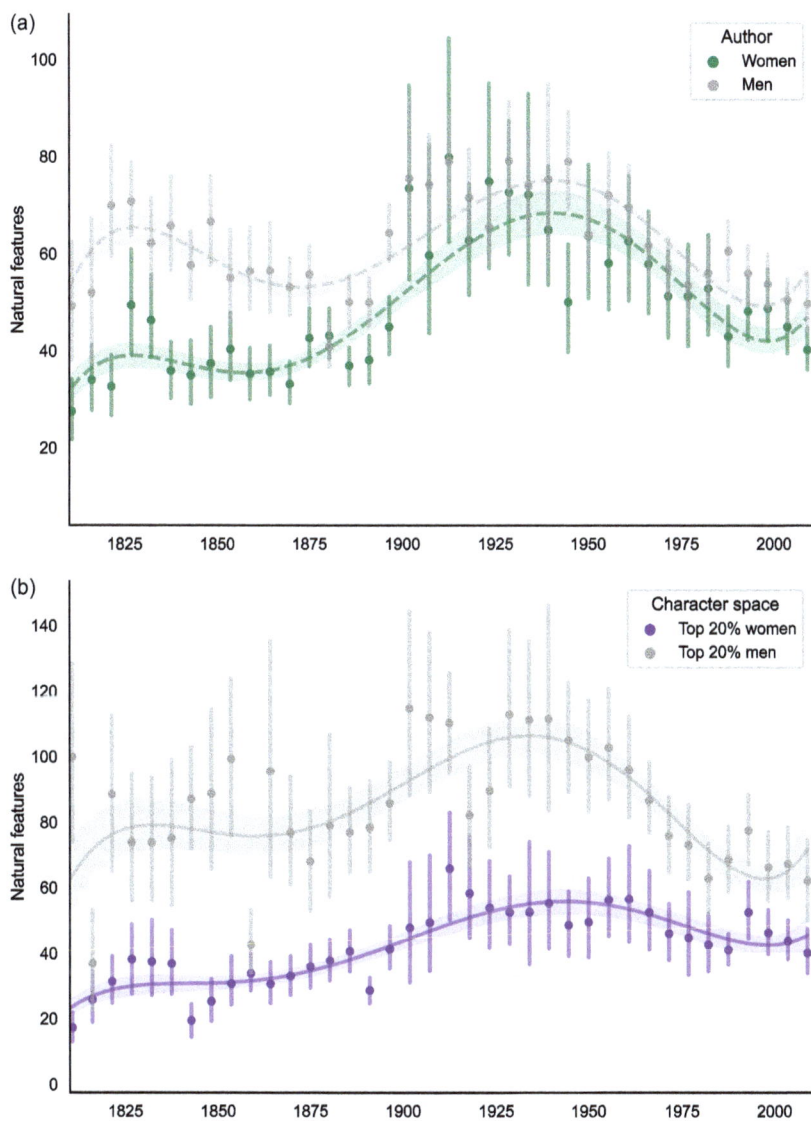

Figure 21 Natural features (a) by author gender and (b) by gendered character space.

river, meadow, and so forth, we found that these natural locations were much more male identified – a startling twice as much when it came to gendered character space (Figure 21(b)).[55] While male authors referenced such places

---

[55] The full list of terms used to identify natural locations is available in the online supplementary materials. As with urban space, we understand natural locations in dialectical relation to human intervention and urban development.

more often, all authors used them most in conjunction with male character space. This identification of men with natural features is surprising in the context of the long-standing association of women with nature and of men with culture, noted in the introduction (see Ortner). It's less surprising if we consider the equally long-standing notion of Nature as a feminine force to be explored and conquered by the male discoverer. (Generic farm and agricultural spaces offer an interesting point of comparison as perhaps another instance of men "taming" nature. Men and women writers represented these spaces at similar rates, while books about men were much more likely to be enriched in such spaces than were women-centered volumes.) Part of the reason for the lower association of male character space with urban locations may thus be the masculine preference of adventure tales – set most often in the wild – and political content, which, as we saw in Section 5, favors national entities.

Let us look more closely at the component parts of the urban metric to better understand our findings. Recall that we assign equal weight to geographical references to cities and the places within them and to references to generic terms associated with urban space. If we look at these two component parts separately, we can see that their gender associations point in different directions: geographic city references were strongly aligned with women authors and women-centered books (Figure 22) while generic terms were (more weakly) correlated with male ones (Figure 23). As we noted in Section 4, there are genre and political differences in the fiction that men and women wrote – and were expected to write. We reason that this accounts for at least some of their different investments in cities. We suspect that the falling off of urban attention in fiction by both groups of authors in the early twentieth century may be an indication of the greater draw of nation-level references in an era of world wars. The relatively flat rate of urban attention in books with character space skewed toward men and toward women poses an interesting contrast. It is not a contradiction, however. Whereas the first figure includes all books in the corpus with an author to whom a gender has been ascribed, the second includes only 20% of each category. It seems that books with more strongly gendered character space were less likely to divert their attention from cities in the early twentieth century.

We see the opposite trend when we look to generic terms associated with the city. Male authors had a greater preference for generic urban terms, especially for the word "street" and its cognates (Figure 23(a)). In books with strongly gendered character space, generic urban terms were greatest in books about men through the nineteenth century, after which the difference disappears (Figure 23 (b)). This correlation between generic urban features and male writers – and, in the nineteenth century, books mostly about men – is difficult to explain. It's

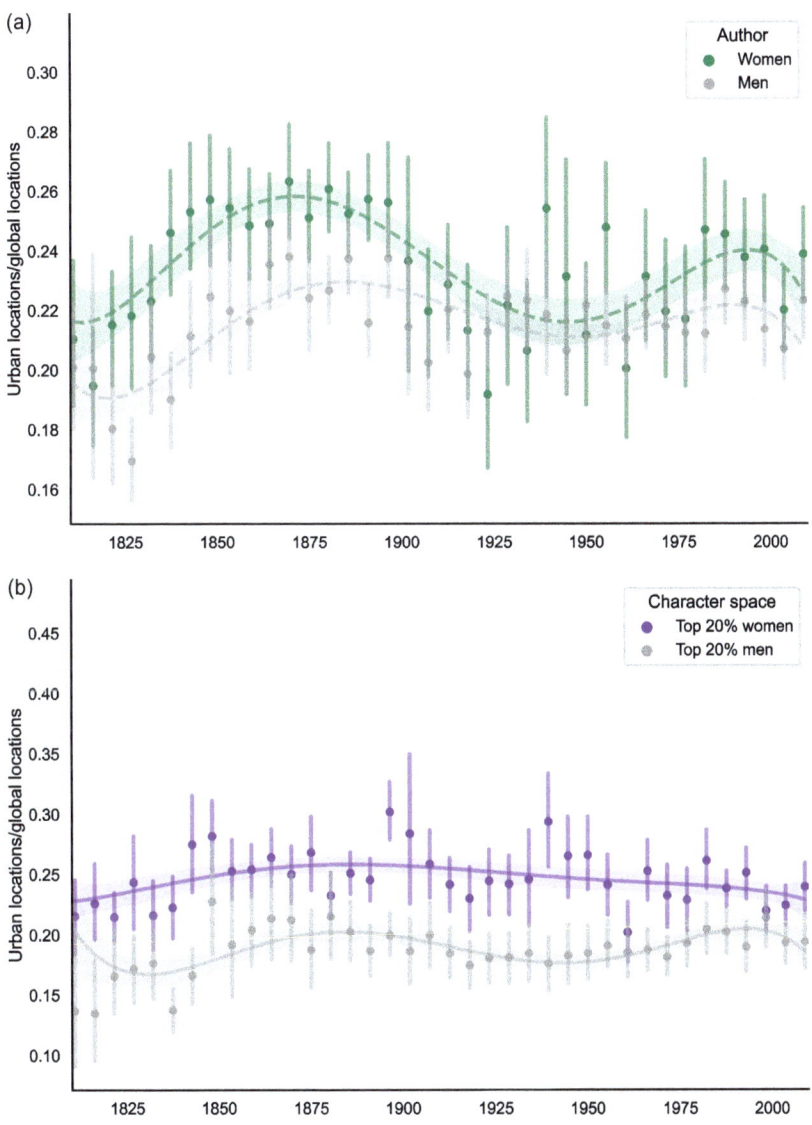

Figure 22 Fraction of geographic references to major cities or places within major cities (a) by author gender and (b) by gendered character space. The vertical axis shows the fraction of all named locations that were urban – roughly 22% across the period.

notable that the difference disappears in twentieth-century gendered character space. The upward trend of words related to urban features is in keeping with the increasing rate of use of most generic terms over time, discussed in Section 6. Indeed, what we might have ascribed to increasing references to urban space, if

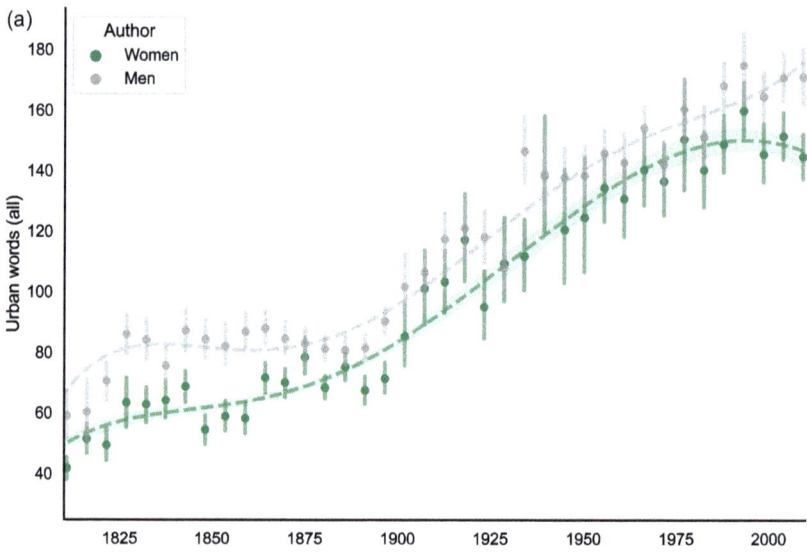

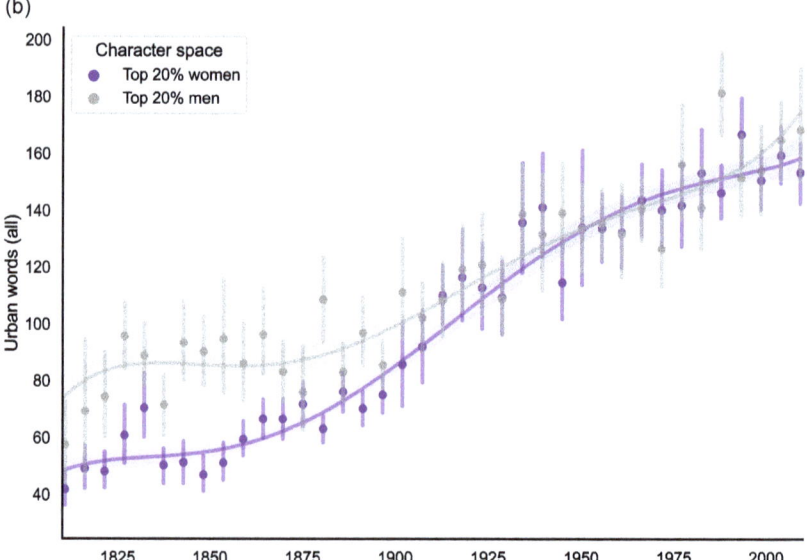

Figure 23 Generic urban terms (a) by author gender and (b) by gendered character space (b). The *y* axis shows the number of references to our set of generic urban terms per 100,000 words.

we had looked only at our urban metric, now appears to be a symptom of broader changes in language use (toward concrete description) rather than a change in the draw of cities.

***

We began this section with three questions through which to investigate whether or not the modern city was represented as a predominantly masculine space, as many critics have claimed. First, we asked to what extent *author gender* predicted the choice of an urban setting. We discovered that men and women authors wrote at similar rates about urban space, but that they did so in different ways. Women authors' references were more often to specific cities and to particular locations within cities, whereas male authors showed a greater preference for generic urban terms – references to streets, vehicles, and crowds that feature so richly in the discourse of flânerie. This suggests that if we look for urban attention through the tropes of flânerie, we may miss other engagements with the city that were more prevalent among women writers.

Our second question was to what extent an urban setting correlated with books that are mostly *about* men or women? We found that books about women were more urban, whether assessed via our urban metric or via geographic references. It is only when we count generic locations alone that the trend is (historically) first reversed and then disappears. If we have not sufficiently observed women's presence in urban writing, it may be because we've been looking at the wrong things. We've certainly been looking at a limited number of texts.

Third, we asked if the modernist era was different from neighboring eras in its representations of gender and the city. We've found that the era was less distinct than scholars have assumed. Indeed, the metropolitan investments that have been in the field since its beginnings turn out not only to be undetectable in fiction at scale but, measured by geographical references, were even in abeyance during the first half of the twentieth century, perhaps as attention turned more to national political entities. The longstanding version of modernism as a masculine metropolitan phenomenon is incorrect, at least when we expand our purview beyond canonical texts. While the city of the high modernists may have leaned male – toward male authors and characters – a wider range of British fiction reveals a much greater association between women and cities than we've known. Indeed, by multiple measures, the city of British fiction was predominantly a space of women.

7.3 Reading Urban Space Anew

In closing, we return to the intersection of women-centered books with those that score highly on the urban metric. We've already mentioned that books by women that were high on the urban metric often focused on women's pursuit of meaningful work and relationships, in contrast to many male-authored tales about women subjugated or corrupted by economic hardship and sexual exploitation in the city. A closer look suggests that women authors were not only choosing different areas of focus than their male counterparts, but were often writing against the paradigm of urban dangers for women.

The title story of Elizabeth Bowen's *The Demon Lover and Other Stories* (1947), which ranked in the top 5% in its urban attention, provides an interesting case study in that the protagonist is in some ways like the desperate women of Gallichan and Burke; she becomes entrapped by a malicious lover. But, while it is an urban tale, set in war-torn London, Bowen makes the roots of sexual danger unplaced, or even quasi pastoral. "The Demon Lover" begins with Mrs. Drover's visit at the end of "her day in London" to the family home that had been boarded up since the family retreated to the country to wait out World War II in relative safety (*Collected Stories*, 661). The house to which she returns in "this quiet, arboreal part of Kensington" (664) is made additionally quiet by many neighbors' similar retreat to the country, so that "no human eye watched Mrs. Drover's return" to her "once familiar street" in which, "as in any unused channel, an unfamiliar queerness had silted up" (661). The deserted city street makes for an uncanny environment that facilitates her abduction by a demon lover who arrives to redeem a vow made in her youth when, twenty-five years earlier, she had pledged herself to a departing soldier in the garden of her parents' home. A taxi – which we saw in Section 6 is often for women the conduit between home spaces and public spaces – is here the vehicle of Mrs. Drover's abduction. While this protagonist does face sexualized danger within an urban environment, the origins of that danger aren't urban and the city in which she's taken is not a bustling metropolis but a "hinterland of deserted streets" (666).

If one method that subverts expectations of urban sexual danger is to ruralize its origins, another is to acknowledge but minimize its threat for the woman protagonist. Dixon's *The Story of a Modern Woman* makes reference to a poor woman who was "the battered leavings of the lust of a great city" (152), but she is not named, nor her story imagined. The heroine's own suffering at the hands of an unscrupulous man takes the form of romantic disappointment, not of urban threats. Indeed, she "stepped along, in the half-dark, with a royal scorn for the well-dressed loafers who find their pleasure in accosting ladies in the street" (67).

Richardson imagines a more overt dismissal of a potential sexual predator in *The Tunnel* when, while walking through a square at night, a man "loomed towards [Miriam] on the narrow pathway and stopped" (96). Miriam's momentary fear, dissipated by the man's "deprecating" manner, is quickly replaced by anger as "She wanted him out of the way and wanted him to know how angry she was at the interruption":

> 'Well,' she snapped angrily, coming to a standstill in the moonlit gap.
> 'Oh,' said the man a little breathlessly in a lame broken tone, 'I thought you were going this way.'
> 'So I am,' retorted Miriam in a loud angry shaking tone, 'obviously.'
> The man stepped quickly into the gutter and walked quickly away across the road. (96)

The passage, and the man's (twice mentioned) quick dispatch, "lame" and "broken," suggests that the biggest danger to Miriam is that such nuisance encounters will deter her from walking at night, for Miriam relishes walking alone at all hours, enjoying the "freedom" of her independent London life (29).

While Bowen displaced urban sexual danger, and Dixon and Richardson relegated it to the margins or minimized it, one of Woolf's tactics was to excise it. Her revisions of the manuscript that would become *The Years* removed most references to sexual danger in the city, including a lengthy passage in which Eleanor Pargiter, walking home after dining alone in an Oxford Street restaurant, changes her path from fear: she was "Afraid to walk through the Park alone" (*Years*, ed. Lee, 465). Elsewhere, in an early version of the manuscript, Woolf commented on how, as young women, the Pargiter girls "could not possibly go for a walk alone ... Bond Street was as impassable, save with their mother, as any swamp alive with crocodiles" (*Pargiters*, 37). It seems likely that Woolf's excisions were a response to how fears for women's safety were often evoked to limit women's freedom of movement.[56] By diminishing representations of women's vulnerability in the city, Woolf made space for other urban stories. The published novel does retain one scene about sexual danger, in which prepubescent Rose is threatened by a strange man on the street when she runs to the corner store after dark. The man moves to expose himself as she runs home, where she is afraid to tell anyone what has happened because she has gone out without permission. The moment is important in Rose's life, but it passes, one among many moments that make up this busy novel. Later references to the adult Rose indicate that she goes on to enjoy the independent life of a modern woman, living with "a friend" (*Years*, 166) and being arrested for throwing a brick (204), presumably as a militant suffragette. Though she remembers the encounter, it did not keep her from – and may have spurred her toward – asserting women's rights to self-determination.

***

---

[56] For a full version of this argument, see Evans, *Threshold Modernism*, 123–30.

In this section, we have found that the city – an environment that has been persistently associated with men – is actually predominantly enriched in women and their experiences when we examine literary production more broadly. We've also seen that the explanation for women's identification with the city is not simple. Male authors often chose women protagonists to explore urban dangers or, alternatively, chose urban spaces to treat women's precarity. Women authors writing about women in urban environments did register, to differing degrees, the dominant cultural narrative about women's sexual endangerment, but found methods of containing it. For them, the city provided women with many possible narratives about the pursuit of personal and professional goals.

8 Conclusions

How to summarize our major findings? They come under three headings. First, there are the findings that directly address our initial questions: what is the geography of British fiction and how does it change in relation to the gender of authors and characters and to the passing of time? Second, there are the findings that are largely incidental to the subject of gender but significant in their own right. These include changes in language use over time and the role of politics in literary geography. Third, we have noted throughout the Element how decisions made in the process of inquiry have shaped the results. What else can we learn about the process of computational analysis as we seek to refine its synergy with close reading?

8.1 Gender and Literary Geography

Some critical commonplaces about nineteenth- and early twentieth-century differences in men and women's relationship with geography were borne out at scale. Male authors and characters were more international in their geographic references and showed greater spatial range than did women authors and characters. We also found support for longstanding associations of women with private space and men with public space, though we noted that semi-public spaces such as vehicles of transport and parks held complex, previously unknown, relationships with gender.

Our findings also departed from critical expectations in significant ways. Contrary to dominant narratives of progress in women's mobility, we found multiple indications of the durability of gendered divisions of space. By many of our measures, the difference between author and character-space gender groups hardly varied over 200 years. There was little evidence of increasing gender parity over time. We also found that, despite the longstanding association of men with urban space, men and women authors referenced city spaces at close to equal rates and books devoted to women *characters* generally made greater use of urban locations (largely as a result of male authors' choices).

One of our most interesting and unexpected findings was that, notwithstanding the urban case, men and women authors were much more similar in their literary geographic attention than were the characters they created. This was the case, for instance, regarding uses of public versus private space and international versus UK locations. Whether because authors were exaggerating for effect the more limited geographic impact of gender in their lives, or because authors made use of geographic and spatial markers to register other kinds of limits to women's access to opportunities, the differences across gendered character space far exceeded those between men and women authors.

We also discovered aspects of gender and geography that we haven't seen considered in previous criticism. We found, for example, that fiction by and about women was often more geographically specific than was fiction by and about men. By a number of measures, including degree of international attention, women writers created more difference between gendered characters than did their male counterparts.

8.2 Politics, Language, Time

Our explorations of gendered geography in relation to conventional periodization underscore the extent to which the books that constitute any workable canon may misrepresent a period's cultural production as a whole. The modernist era broadly considered, for instance, was no more cosmopolitan than other periods and was a good deal less international than was the late nineteenth century, despite critical commonplaces to the contrary. As computational literary history has sometimes emphasized, stability over time is an understudied aspect of cultural production.

We also documented changes in language use over time, such as the increased use of generic spatial terms and a shift in the meaning of "the nation" in British fiction from England and the other Home Nations to the UK and Great Britain. We saw the intersection of geography with major political events – how, for instance, world wars aligned with changes to the proportion of locations that were international, though perhaps not to the extent that one might have expected. Empire had surprisingly small geographic impacts in literature while it was at its administrative peak.

Finally, we saw that the imaginative map of the literary world expanded at a relatively steady rate between the early nineteenth century and the late twentieth, so that the average book today has about three times the geographic range as did one published two centuries ago.

8.3 Hybrid Methods

We have discussed historical patterns and used case studies to demonstrate how computational results can reshape our understanding of individual texts. We hope that by foregrounding the decisions we made along the way, readers have been able to consider the range of options available and their probable impact on findings. Computational research, no less than traditional methods of literary study, calls for a combination of logic and creativity.

We highlight here four methodological aspects of our research that we believe contain lessons for future work in the field. First, the scale enabled by computation goes some way toward addressing problems of representation in literary studies, even as it raises new issues. Our corpus of over 20,000 volumes is large; it includes stories and voices that are excluded from much conventional criticism. There is every reason to believe that it captures more usefully the sum of literary production in Britain over two centuries than might any readable set of novels, no matter how carefully chosen. But our corpus is not equivalent to British literature; it is a *representation* of British literature. We have tried to be direct about the affordances and limitations of that representation. Other corpora, drawn from other sources, assembled for different purposes, and curated according to different principles, will produce competing and complementary representations. Each of these will be more productive for some purposes than for others. No one of them will be correct, because there is no such thing as a correct representation of a national literature.

Second, we highlight the need for, and the difficulty of, devising suitable metrics for the concepts in which we are interested. This is not a challenge unique to computational work, but it receives perhaps more direct attention when we are confronted by the need to translate our ideas into code.[57] The claim that women historically faced greater restrictions on their mobility than did men, and that this fact was reflected in literature, raises as many questions as it answers. We have tried to be explicit about our modeling choices, from how we assess the gender composition of a book, to the many ways in which we measure mobility, to what we mean by public and private space. It is our sense that criticism in general would not be harmed by greater explicitness, if only because all criticism is at some level quantitative (noting the prominence or recurrence of a particular feature or device, for example). Critics always model, and they always count. Let us explain our choices, so that we do not assume we all count the same things in the same ways.

Third, our analysis, like much of the research we admire, attempts to move between large-scale quantification and detailed qualitative explanation. This is

---

[57] See also Moretti, "Operationalizing."

not a new point; calls for "scalable" reading (Martin Mueller's term) have existed for decades. We add only that scalable reading is not a matter of finding the same results by different means, because the patterns that we recognize at different scales are not simply extensions of one another. We do not measure shared features over 20,000 books that are usefully illustrated in a passage or two from a single novel, even if it can be helpful to consider individual novels that are typical with respect to that feature. Instead, we offer qualitative analyses of the quantitative results themselves; the numbers are the objects of interpretive attention, though the analysis as a whole ultimately serves a cultural argument. When we read a novel, we do so in light of our quantitative findings not to further substantiate any statistical claim but to produce a different kind of knowledge about the books. We note that quantitative work does not always require this complement, just as qualitative analysis does not always require computation.

Finally, a word on the road ahead. The landscape of computational approaches to textual analysis is evolving at a startling rate. When we first conceived this study, the technology that underpins generative artificial intelligence was in its infancy. Today, an AI-based system would be the obvious starting point for an analogous project. For the reasons we summarized in Section 3 (including but not limited to cost, collaborative complexity, copyright issues, the need for human interaction, and the ongoing interplay of established and novel evidence), there is no suggestion that AI systems will "solve" criticism or replace literary critics. But these systems are already extending the range of what critics can accomplish.

We want to close, then, with an invitation to explore this augmented range. Where natural language processing was once the nearly exclusive purview of linguists and computer scientists, and while the analysis of quantitative results continues to demand experience and technical knowledge, the systems themselves have become very easy to use. Generative AI can respond in natural language to textual inputs in multiple human languages via a web page. All of the lessons about care, explicitness, and rigor still apply, but the barriers to exploration in the field have never been lower. When more people can join the community of computational critical work, both criticism and computation will benefit.

Bibliography

Adorno, Theodor and Max Horkheimer. *Dialectic of Enlightenment* (1947), Palo Alto: Stanford University Press, 2007.

Algee-Hewitt, Mark, Sarah Allison, Marissa Gemma, et al. "Canon/Archive: Large-Scale Dynamics in the Literary Field," *Pamphlets of the Stanford Literary Lab*, 11 (2016).

Armstrong, Nancy. *Desire and Domestic Fiction: A Political History of the Novel*, Oxford: Oxford University Press, 1987.

Bakhtin, Mikhail. *The Dialogic Imagination: Four Essays* (1934–41; 1975). Ed. Michael Holquist. Trans. Caryl Emerson and Michael Holquist. Austin: University of Texas Press, 1981.

Bamman, David, Sejal Popat, and Sheng Shen. "An Annotated Dataset of Literary Entities," in *Proceedings of the 2019 Conference of the North American Chapter of the Association for Computational Linguistics*, Vol. 1, Minneapolis, MN: Association for Computational Linguistics, 2019, 2138–44.

Bamman, David, Ted Underwood, and Noah A. Smith, "A Bayesian Mixed Effects Model of Literary Character," in *Proceedings of the 52nd Annual Meeting of the Association for Computational Linguistics*. Baltimore: Association for Computational Linguistics, 2014, 370–79.

Berman, Marshall. *All That Is Solid Melts into Air: The Experience of Modernity* (1982), New York: Penguin Books, 1988.

Bluemel, Kristin and Michael McCluskey, eds. *Rural Modernity in Britain: A Critical Intervention*, Edinburgh: Edinburgh University Press, 2018.

Bogart, Dan, Xuesheng You, Eduard J. Alvarez-Palau, Max Satchell, and Leigh Shaw-Taylor. "Railways, Divergence, and Structural Change in 19th Century England and Wales," *Journal of Urban Economics* 128 (2022): 1–23.

Bowen, Elizabeth. *The Collected Stories of Elizabeth Bowen*, New York: Anchor Books, 2006.

Buck-Morss, Susan. "The Flaneur, the Sandwichman, and the Whore," *New German Critique* 39 (1986): 99–140.

Brown, Susan and Laura Mandell. "The Identity Issue," *Journal of Cultural Analytics* 1.1 (2018): 1–18.

Conrad, Joseph. *The Secret Agent* (1907), ed. Martin Seymour-Smith, New York: Penguin, 1984.

Cooper, David, Christopher Donaldson, and Patricia Murrieta-Flores, eds. *Literary Mapping in the Digital Age*, London: Routledge, 2016.

Dawson, Ashley. *Mongrel Nation: Diasporic Culture and the Making of Postcolonial Britain*, Ann Arbor: University of Michigan Press, 2007.

Dixon, Ella Hepworth. *The Story of a Modern Woman* (1894), ed. Steve Farmer. Peterborough: Broadview, 2004.

Duplessis, Rachel Blau. *Writing beyond the Ending: Narrative Strategies of Twentieth-Century Women Writers*, Bloomington: Indiana University Press, 1985.

Edelstein, Dan, Paula Findlen, Nicole Coleman, and Giovanna Ceserani. "Historical Research in a Digital Age: Reflections from the Mapping the Republic of Letters Project," *The American Historical Review* 122.2 (2017): 400–24.

Elkin, Lauren. *Flâneuse: Women Walk the City in Paris, New York, Tokyo, Venice, and London*. New York: Farrar, Straus and Giroux, 2017.

Engel, Laura and Emily Ruth Rutter. "Women and Archives," *Tulsa Studies in Women's Literature* 40.1 (2021): 5–13.

Evans, Elizabeth F. "Alternative Geographies and Urban Parks: Duse Mohamed Ali and Yoshio Markino in Imperial London," *ELH*, in press.

Evans, Elizabeth F. "The Promises and Limits of Virginia Woolf's London Parks," in *Virginia Woolf and Transnationalism*, ed. Shinjini Chattopadhyay. Edinburgh University Press, in press.

Evans, Elizabeth F. *Threshold Modernism: New Public Women and the Literary Spaces of Imperial London*, Cambridge: Cambridge University Press, 2019.

Evans, Elizabeth F. and Matthew Wilkens. "Nation, Ethnicity, and the Geography of British Fiction, 1880–1940," *Journal of Cultural Analytics* 3.2 (2018): 1–48.

Felski, Rita. *The Gender of Modernity*, Cambridge, MA: Harvard University Press, 1995.

Fernald, Anne. "Taxi! The Modern Taxicab as Feminist Heterotopia," *Modernist Cultures* 9.2 (2014): 213–32.

Finkel, Jenny Rose, Trond Grenager, and Christopher Manning. "Incorporating Non-local Information into Information Extraction Systems by Gibbs Sampling," in *Proceedings of the 43nd Annual Meeting of the Association for Computational Linguistics (ACL 2005)*, Ann Arbor: Association for Computational Linguistics, 2005: 363–70.

Friedman, Susan Stanford. *Mappings: Feminism and the Cultural Geographies of Encounter*, Princeton, NJ: Princeton University Press, 1998.

Gavin, Adrienne E. and Andrew F. Humphries, eds. *Transport in British Fiction: Technologies of Movement, 1840–1940*, London: Palgrave Macmillan, 2015.

Gilbert, Sandra and Susan Gubar. *The Madwoman in the Attic: The Woman Writer and the Nineteenth-Century Literary Imagination*, New Haven, CT: Yale University Press, 1979.

Gilroy, Paul. *The Black Atlantic: Modernity and Double Consciousness*, Cambridge, MA: Harvard University Press, 1993.

Gleber, Anke. *The Art of Taking a Walk: Flanerie, Literature, and Film in Weimar Culture*, Princeton, NJ: Princeton University Press, 1999.

GoGwilt, Chris. "The Interior: Benjaminian Arcades, Conradian Passages, and the 'Impasse' of Jean Rhys," in *Geographies of Modernism: Literatures, Cultures, Spaces*, eds. Peter Brooker and Andrew Thacker, London: Routledge, 2005: 65–75.

Grossman, Jonathan. *Charles Dickens's Networks: Public Transport and the Novel*, Oxford: Oxford University Press, 2012.

Hall, Radclyffe. *Miss Ogilvy Finds Herself*, London: William Heinemann, 1934.

Heuser, Ryan and Long Le-Khak. "A Quantitative Literary History of 2,958 Nineteenth-Century British Novels: The Semantic Cohort Method," *Pamphlets of the Stanford Literary Lab* 4 (2012).

Hubble, Nick and Philip Tew, eds. *London in Contemporary British Fiction*, London: Bloomsbury, 2016.

Jameson, Fredric. "Modernism and Imperialism." Reprinted as chapter 7 of *The Modernist Papers*. New York: Verso, 2007. First published, under the same title, as Field Day pamphlet no. 14 (1988) and collected in *Nationalism, Colonialism, and Literature*, ed. Seamus Deane. Minneapolis, MN: University of Minnesota Press, 1990, 43–66.

Jett, Jacob, Boris Capitanu, Deren Kudeki et al. *The HathiTrust Research Center Extracted Features Dataset (2.0)*. HathiTrust Research Center.

Jockers, Matthew and Gabi Kiriloff, "Understanding Gender and Character Agency in the 19th Century Novel," *Journal of Cultural Analytics* 2.2 (2017): 1–26.

Kelley, Joyce. *Excursions into Modernism: Women Writers, Travel, and the Body*, New York: Routledge, 2016.

Kiberd, Declan. *Inventing Ireland: The Literature of the Modern Nation*, Cambridge, MA: Harvard University Press, 1997.

Lafferty, John D., Andrew McCallum, and Fernando C. N. Pereira. "Conditional Random Fields: Probabilistic Models for Segmenting and Labeling Sequence Data." *Proceedings of the Eighteenth International Conference on Machine Learning (ICML '01)*, San Francisco, CA: Morgan Kaufmann, 2001: 282–89.

Lawrence, Karen R. *Penelope Voyages: Women and Travel in the British Literary Tradition*, Ithaca, NY: Cornell University Press, 1988.

Lessing, Doris. *The Golden Notebook*, New York: Harper Collins, 2008.

Massey, Doreen. *Space, Place, and Gender*, Minneapolis, MN: University of Minnesota Press, 1994.

Moretti, Franco. *Graphs, Maps, Trees: Abstract Models for Literary History*. London: Verso, 2005.

Moretti, Franco. "Operationalizing, or, the Function of Measurement in Literary Theory," *New Left Review* 84 (2013): 103–19.

Mullen, John. "Railways in Victorian Fiction," *Technical Report of the British Library*, 2014. np.

Mullholland, Terri. *British Boarding Houses in Interwar Women's Literature: Alternative Domestic Spaces*, London: Routledge, 2017.

Nead, Lynda. *Victorian Babylon: People, Streets and Images in Nineteenth-Century London*, New Haven, CT: Yale University Press, 2000.

Nord, Deborah Epstein. *Walking the Victorian Streets: Women, Representation and the City*, Ithaca, NY: Cornell University Press, 1995.

Ortner, Sherry B. "Is Female to Male as Nature Is to Culture?" *Feminist Studies* 1.2 (1972): 5–31.

Parkins, Wendy. *Mobility and Modernity in Women's Novels, 1850s–1930s: Women Moving Dangerously*, London: Palgrave Macmillan, 2008.

Parsons, Deborah L. *Street Walking the Metropolis: Women, the City and Modernity*, Oxford: Oxford University Press, 2000.

Peach, Linden. "'Re-reading Sickert's Interiors': Woolf, English Art and the Representation of Domestic Space," *Locating Woolf: The Politics of Space and Place*, eds. Anna Snaith and Michael H. Whitworth, London: Palgrave Macmillan, 2007: 65–80.

Piper, Andrew. *Enumerations: Data and Literary Study*, Chicago, IL: University of Chicago Press, 2018.

Ranasinha, Ruvani. *Contemporary Diasporic South Asian Women's Fiction: Gender, Narration and Globalisation*, New York: Palgrave Macmillan, 2016.

Rhys, Jean. *Voyage in the Dark* (1934), New York: W.W. Norton, 1982.

Richardson, Dorothy. *The Tunnel* (1919) *(Pilgrimage, Vol. II)*, London: Virago, 1992.

Ryan, Yann C. and Sebastian E. Ahnert, "The Measure of the Archive: The Robustness of Network Analysis in Early Modern Correspondence," *Journal of Cultural Analytics* 7 (2021): 57–88.

Sanders, Lise Shapiro. *Consuming Fantasies: Labor, Leisure, and the London Shopgirl, 1880–1920*, Columbus: Ohio State University Press, 2006.

Shiach, Morag. "Modernism, the City and the 'Domestic Interior,'" *Home Cultures* 2.3 (2005): 251–68.

Snaith, Anna. *Modernist Voyages: Colonial Women Writers in London, 1890–1945*, Cambridge: Cambridge University Press, 2014.

Snaith, Anna. *Virginia Woolf: Public and Private Negotiations*, London: Palgrave Macmillan, 2000.

Soni, Sandeep, Amanpreet Sihra, Elizabeth F. Evans, Matthew Wilkens, and David Bamman. "Grounding Characters and Places in Narrative Text," in *Proceedings of the 61st Annual Meeting of the Association for Computational Linguistics (ACL'23)*. Toronto: Association for Computational Linguistics (2023): 11723–736.

Stokes, John. "'Encabsulation': Horse-Drawn Journeys in Late-Victorian Literature," *Journal of Victorian Culture* 15.2 (2010): 239–53.

Thacker, Andrew. *Moving through Modernity: Space and Geography in Modernism*, Manchester: Manchester University Press, 2003.

Underwood, Ted. *Distant Horizons: Digital Evidence and Literary Change*, Chicago, IL: University of Chicago Press, 2019.

Underwood, Ted. "Understanding Genre in a Collection of a Million Volumes," Interim Performance Report, NEH Digital Humanities Start-Up Grant. 29 December, 2014.

Underwood, Ted, David Bamman, and Sabrina Lee, "The Transformation of Gender in English-Language Fiction," *Journal of Cultural Analytics* 3.2 (2018): 1–25.

Underwood, Ted, Patrick Kimutis, and Jessica Witte, "NovelTM Datasets for English-Language Fiction, 1700–2009," *Journal of Cultural Analytics* 5.2 (2020): 1–30.

Underwood, Ted and Jordan Sellers. "The Emergence of Literary Diction," *Journal of Digital Humanities* 1.2 (2012).

Vadillo, Ana Parejo. *Women Poets and Urban Aestheticism: Passengers of Modernity*, London: Palgrave Macmillan, 2005.

Vicinus, Martha. *Independent Women: Work and Community for Single Women, 1850–1920*, Chicago, IL: University of Chicago Press, 1985.

Walker, Lynn. "Locating the Global/Rethinking the Local: Suffrage Politics, Architecture, and Space," *Women's Studies Quarterly* 34.1–2 (2006): 174–96.

Walkowitz, Judith. *City of Dreadful Delight: Narratives of Sexual Danger in London*, London: Virago, 1992.

Wilkens, Matthew. "'Too Isolated, Too Insular': American Fiction and the World," *Journal of Cultural Analytics* 6 (2021): 52–84.

Wilkens, Matthew. "Literary Attention Lag," *Work Product*, 2015.

Wilkens, Matthew. *Textual Geographies*. txtgeo.net.

Wilkens, Matthew, Elizabeth F. Evans, Sandeep Soni, and David Bamman. "Small Worlds: Measuring the Mobility of Characters in English-Language Fiction," *Journal of Computational Literary Studies* 3.1 (2024), 1–16.

Wilson, Elizabeth. "The Invisible Flâneur," *New Left Review* 191 (1992): 90–110.

Wolff, Janet. "The Invisible Flâneuse: Women and the Literature of Modernity," *Theory, Culture & Society* 2.3 (1985): 37–46.

Woloch, Alex. *The One Versus the Many: Minor Characters and the Space of the Protagonist in the Novel*, Princeton, NJ: Princeton University Press, 2003.

Wolff, Janet. "The Invisible Flâneuse: Women and the Literature of Modernity," *Theory, Culture, and Society* 2.3 (1985): 37–46.

Woolf, Virginia. *Mrs. Dalloway* (1925), New York: Harcourt Brace Jovanovich, 1981.

Woolf, Virginia. *The Pargiters: The Novel-Essay Portion of the Years*, ed. and intro. Mitchell A. Leaska, London: Hogarth Press, 1978.

Woolf, Virginia. *The Years* (1937), New York: Harcourt Brace, 1965.

Woolf, Virginia. *The Years*, ed. and intro. Hermione Lee, Oxford: Oxford University Press, 1992.

Zink, Suzana. *Woolf's Rooms and the Spaces of Modernity*, London: Palgrave Macmillan, 2018.

Online Supplement

Supplementary materials, including code, derived data, corpus listings, and additional visualizations are available at www.cambridge.org/EvansWilkens.

Acknowledgement

This research was supported by the National Endowment for the Humanities via grants HK-250673–16 and HAA-290374–23 to Mathew Wilkens. Elizabeth F. Evans received funding from Wayne State University through a Career Development Chair, 2022–23, and from the Wayne State University Humanities Center as a Resident Scholar, 2021–22, and as a 2024 Summer Faculty Fellow. We are grateful for their support. We also gratefully acknowledge the Helen Riaboff Whiteley Center in Friday Harbor, Washington, for positions to both authors as Researchers in Residence, July 2024. Finally, we thank Stella Deen, Megan Faragher, and the anonymous reviewers for their generous and helpful engagement with drafts of the manuscript.

We dedicate this work to Calliope and Theodore.

Cambridge Elements

Digital Literary Studies

Katherine Bode
Australian National University

Katherine Bode is Professor of Literary and Textual Studies at the Australian National University. Her research explores the critical potential and limitations of computational approaches to literature, in publications including *A World of Fiction: Digital Collections and the Future of Literary History* (2018), *Advancing Digital Humanities: Research, Methods, Theories* (2014), *Reading by Numbers: Recalibrating the Literary Field* (2012), and *Resourceful Reading: The New Empiricism, eResearch and Australian Literary Culture* (2009).

Adam Hammond
University of Toronto

Adam Hammond is Assistant Professor of English at the University of Toronto. He is author of *Literature in the Digital Age* (Cambridge 2016) and co-author of *Modernism: Keywords* (2014). He works on modernism, digital narrative, and computational approaches to literary style. He is editor of the forthcoming *Cambridge Companion to Literature in the Digital Age* and *Cambridge Critical Concepts: Literature and Technology*.

Gabriel Hankins
Clemson University

Gabriel Hankins is Associate Professor of English at Clemson University. His first book is *Interwar Modernism and the Liberal World Order* (Cambridge 2019). He writes on modernism, digital humanities, and color. He is technical manager for the Twentieth Century Literary Letters Project and co-editor on *The Digital Futures of Graduate Study in the Humanities* (in progress).

Advisory Board

David Bammen *University of California, Berkeley*
Amy Earhardt *Texas A&M University*
Dirk Van Hulle *University of Oxford*
Fotis Jannidis *Julius-Maximilians-Universität*
Matthew Kirschenbaum *University of Maryland*
Laura Mandell *Texas A&M University*
Élika Ortega-Guzman *University of Colorado, Boulder*
Marisa Parham *Amherst College*
Rita Raley *University of California, Santa Barbara*
Scott Rettberg *University of Bergen*
Roopika Risam *Salem State University*
Glenn Roe *Sorbonne University*
Whitney Trettien *University of Pennsylvania*
Ted Underwood *University of Illinois*

About the Series

Our series provides short exemplary texts that address a pressing research question of clear scholarly interest within a defined area of literary studies, clearly articulate the method used to address the question, and demonstrate the literary insights achieved.

Cambridge Elements

Digital Literary Studies

Elements in the Series

Can We Be wrong? The Problem of Textual Evidence in a Time of Data
Andrew Piper

Literary Geographies in Balzac and Proust
Melanie Conroy

The Shapes of Stories: Sentiment Analysis for Narrative
Katherine Elkins

Actual Fictions: Literary Representation and Character Network Analysis
Roel Smeets

The Challenges of Born-Digital Fiction: Editions, Translations, and Emulations
Dene Grigar and Mariusz Pisarski

New Approaches for Digital Literary Mapping: Chronotopic Cartography
Sally Bushell and Rebecca Hutcheon

Gender and Literary Geography
Elizabeth F. Evans and Matthew Wilkens

A full series listing is available at: www.cambridge.org/EDLS

For EU product safety concerns, contact us at Calle de José Abascal, 56–1°,
28003 Madrid, Spain or eugpsr@cambridge.org.

www.ingramcontent.com/pod-product-compliance
Ingram Content Group UK Ltd.
Pitfield, Milton Keynes, MK11 3LW, UK
UKHW021345150525
458466UK00017B/106